This book is dedicated to

Margaret Carmody Lang

whose personal strength, faith and character
has been shared by millions of
wives, parents and lovers
during periods of national conflict.

Other books by Norman Rudi

An Iowa Pilot Named Hap
2001

A Neighborhood of Eagles
2003

LANG

The WWII Story of An American Guerrilla on Mindanao, Philippine Islands

By NORMAN RUDI

Published, printed and distributed by:

McMillen
Publishing.
A Sigler Company

Library of Congress Control Number: Pending

ISBN: 1-888223-52-9

www.mcmillenbooks.com

All opinions expressed herein are solely those of the author or subjects and do not necessarily reflect those of McMillen Publishing.

Editor's note: Text written by subjects (letters, logs, etc.) are mostly unedited so as to preserve the integrity of the writing; any inconsistencies in spelling, capitalization, style, etc., have been left intentionally.

First Lieutenant Dick Lang in a picture taken the month he returned to the United States.

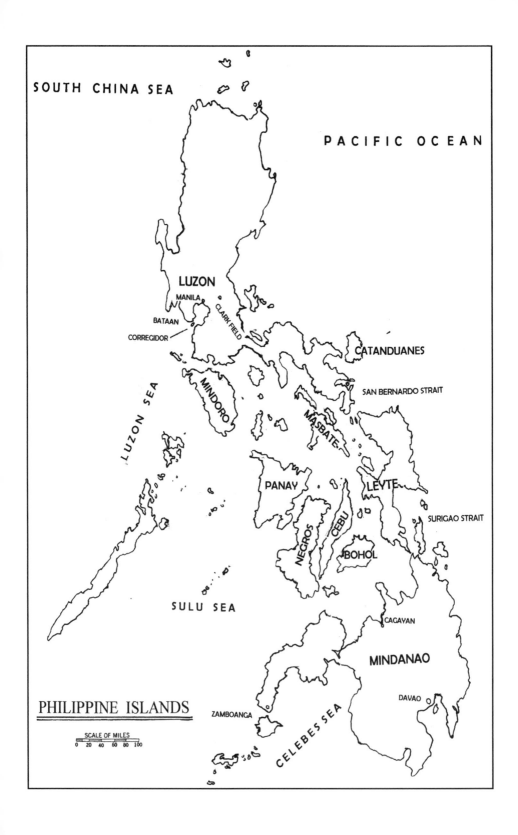

SOUTH CHINA SEA

PACIFIC OCEAN

LUZON

MANILA

BATAAN

CORREGIDOR

CLARK FIELD

CATANDUANES

SAN BERNARDO STRAIT

LUZON SEA

MINDORO

MASBATE

PANAY

LEYTE

SURIGAO STRAIT

NEGROS

CEBU

BOHOL

SULU SEA

CAGAYAN

MINDANAO

DAVAO

PHILIPPINE ISLANDS

ZAMBOANGA

CELEBES SEA

SCALE OF MILES
0 20 40 60 80 100

TABLE OF CONTENTS

INTRODUCTION

Imagine putting down this book, getting out of your chair, and walking out the front door into a jungle, where you will subsist for over two years with what you have with you. What are the conveniences of necessity you will miss the most? Make a list of those items we take for granted, that would make our life unbearably uncomfortable without. Would the list include: toothpaste, toilet paper, eating utensils, soap, hand towels, salt and pepper, dry stockings, a calendar, a knife, drinking water, matches, electricity?

The prospect is rather intimidating, even in today's world. In the last sixty years, our civilization has responded to our every whim, desire, and frivolous pursuit. We tend to overlook those basic items that in reality make our life comfortable. In 1941, the options were limited.

When Dick Lang entered the jungle, not only were environmental conditions unfriendly, but the enemy and some of the local inhabitants, plus disease, added to their unknown peril. When survival is at stake, a whole new attitude prevails.

War in the Southwest Pacific is difficult to comprehend. The emphasis on the international conflict centered in Europe. It received the most news ink, since more of our forbearers originated from there, but also because members of the press found living conditions far more civil in London's hotels. The Army and Air Corps were more highly involved in Europe since they had a stable base to work from, called England.

Fighting in the Southwest Pacific required more water transportation to disseminate supplies and personnel. Members of the United States Naval staffs and Army staffs were still involved in a command power struggle when the Japanese bombed Pearl Harbor and the Philippine Islands. As a result, they were little prepared to withstand attack and invasion in the early stages of the war. The few military resources available were not properly utilized in preparation for defensive or offensive advantage.

The Japanese military had been active for over a decade, preparing to expand their empire to acquire material resources necessary to sustain their grand scheme. The middle 1930's saw Japan invade China and Manchuria, which helped to develop their military mindset for later application. Their intricate planning and distribution of military capability to accomplish their expansion during the end of 1941 and first six months of 1942 was remarkable. In spite of their treachery of unprovoked attack, the success of their military conquests must be acknowledged.

In order for America to rebuild and respond required a highly concentrated effort to recover from the disasters experienced in December of 1941. The United States' isolation from direct conflict enabled planners and logicians to respond to the big picture. The expansion of manufacturing capability was not hindered by military battles or physical intrusions. The only impedance to organize and produce the material to wage war was the chaos of establishing priorities and the enthusiasm "to do our part."

Many isolated victims caught in the forefront of Japan's expansion and were unprepared for being thrust in a role to simply survive. The people of the Philippine Islands were particularly destabilized because of the geology of their islands, lack of communication and the far-flung political diversity caused by a number of historical precedents. The Filipinos virtues of resilience, family centricity, and adaptability helped them to survive, even though subjected to atrocities difficult for the western mind to imagine.

The American soldiers, who were also isolated victims in the forefront of Japan's expansion, responded in several different ways. Those who fought a defensive battle in Bataan and ultimately surrendered suffered humiliation and death in the hands of their Japanese conquerors in several prison camps throughout the islands.

Many soldiers chose not to surrender to the Japanese as ordered to do, and entered the jungle in an attempt to find a way to get to Australia where they could return to perform their military duties.

These soldiers put down their book, got out of their easy chair, and walked through the front door into the jungle where for over two years they learned to subsist, adapt, and survive. They confronted hunger, disease, and a raw harsh environment. They learned that working together, many obstacles can be overcome, and the difficult can be accomplished.

This is one person's story of walking through that door into the jungle.

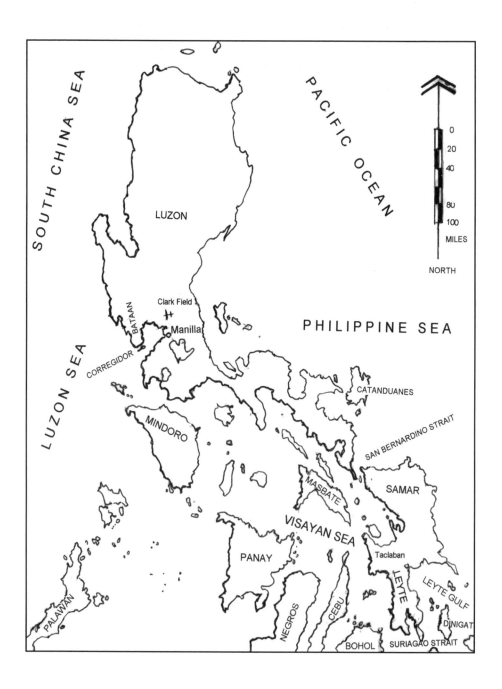

Chapter One

CLARK FIELD

The bolo knife chopped through the palmetto fronds and pandana stalks making crude ragged cuts through the tough fibers. Every slash at the sinewy stalks disturbed infestations of small gnats that swarmed about, sticking to the hot sweaty bodies of the maintenance crew as they moved about under the bright sun. Humidity and temperature caused sweat to run down from the temples, and shirts were wet to the waist. Branches from nearby talisay trees were leaned against the fuselage, and palmetto fronds placed against the body and on the wings of the grounded bomber, in a crude attempt to camouflage the huge aircraft. Concealing a B-17 was difficult at best, and the eight maintenance men grumbled, sweat and swore as they carried the dirty, dusty jungle plants on this December morning.

Thirty-five B-17s arrived a few days earlier at Clark Field, Luzon from the Hawaiian Islands. The big bombers were immediately swarmed upon by the maintenance men of the 19th Bombardment Group for the servicing necessary to return them to the air. All of the planes needed some degree of repair, and one needed engine changes. Fifteen of the Fortresses took off at 9:30 am and flew to Mindanao Island, one thousand miles further south. The remaining planes were neatly aligned along the runway with military precision, as maintenance crews performed last minute testing. The fifty-five P-40 "Warhawk" fighter planes and a few other miscellaneous aircraft were positioned in the same manner, their bright aluminum bodies glistening in the early morning sun. The planes, in the process of being painted a camouflage green, were patiently waiting their turn for a trip to the paint shop.

Private First Class Dick Lang and members of the maintenance team continued their attempt to conceal the B-17 with four missing engines sitting at the end of the runway. They continued to sweat and swear, chop and carry.

Colonel Eubank, the base commander, attended a staff meeting in Manila and returned at 11:30 am. He wanted his B-17 ready to leave for Australia by mid-afternoon. Lang, up early, had a big breakfast in the mess building, and was on his way to the flight line at 6:00 am to give the Colonel's 17 a thorough pre-flight inspection. As Dick and Tony Haratik left the mess and walked down the hardstand approaching the flight line, a soldier on guard duty stopped them.

"The Officer of the Day was just by," the guard said. "Seems the Japs bombed Pearl Harbor this morning."

"Pearl?"

" Yeah, Pearl. Don't think they'll try anything here. The OD said if I saw anyone going to the flight line, tell 'em if Jap planes showed up to use the plane's machine guns on them."

"Pearl?"

"The navy at Pearl would give the Japs a kick in the butt."

"I'll be damned. I thought those lectures about the Japs were just to keep us busy," Dick commented as they walked on.

A few days after their arrival at Clark Field, on Luzon in the Philippine Islands, Group Commander Colonel Eubanks called the soldiers together. He explained the tense situation in the far Pacific and the need to keep their airplanes in top condition. He felt the Air Corps was the only defense the islands really had since the Navy was committed to other areas of the Pacific. Being Americans, he thought our airplanes would be enough to win a war or at least stop the Japanese from starting one. He did not think the Japanese would have the nerve to start anything.

As a precaution, the Colonel had them dig foxholes, practice alerts, add blackout curtains to building windows, and assigned defense duties. The last days of November were spent preparing for the arrival of the new B-17 bombers and digging foxholes, pits and L-shaped trenches that probably never would be needed.

The maintenance crew was nearly complete with the bomber's pre-flight, when a number of the P-40 "Warhawks" responded to an alert, taxied to the hardstand and raced down the runway. They formed a triple "Vee" formation and headed west.

A jeep carrying the Officer of the Day stopped by and directed Lang and the crew to cut jungle brush to camouflage a grounded B-17 with missing engines at one end of the runway. The men groused as they rounded up several bolo knifes and commenced the hot and difficult task. "Why a grounded airplane? This stuff is sticky and dirty." "Why the hell don't we have netting?" "Whose dumb idea was this?" They continued to hack, carry and sweat until the plane was fairly well concealed.

Around 11:30 am the Warhawks returned and taxied to their spot with "dress right" precision. With the alert canceled, plane crews and maintenance men headed for the mess hall. Since Colonel Eubanks was preparing to leave, assistant crew chief Lang and several of his maintenance team took their sweaty bodies back to the flight line to work on Colonel Eubank's B-17.

Lang was standing on a ladder cleaning the plastic nose windows when one of the maintenance crew, Olin Light, pointed out a formation of planes approaching the field. "Are we expecting more planes? With that tight a formation, it must be navy planes!"

"I count over fifty. Hell, we don't have that many planes."

Suddenly, small shiny objects descended from the overhead formations. Sixty-seven Mitsubishi 21 IIe two-engine bombers released their bomb load from 10,000 feet, hitting the maintenance shops, hangars and service buildings. The men jumped from the B-17 and headed for nearby foxholes as the bombs continued to drop, all making it safely. Dust and debris flew from the runway, but most of the runway was still useable. Pilots, staff and maintenance crews tumbled out of the mess hall and headed for their stations. A few pilots managed to get to their P-40s, racing down the runway to get airborne in pursuit of the Jap bombers.

As the Mitsubishis completed their bombing run and headed back to their home base, formations of Zero fighter planes appeared and strafed the rows of bombers and fighters neatly aligned as easy targets. Eighty Zeros shot at everything in sight with minimal opposition from the Americans. The Warhawks that did get airborne faced overwhelming odds, but managed to shoot down four Zeros before becoming the first fighting casualties of air war in the Philippines. Planes on the ground were in shambles as the Zeros made pass after pass, and a grass fire ignited from the action. Fire spread through the dry coogan grass around the foxholes, creeping toward the fortresses.

Lang surveyed the carnage. "Let's move the Colonel's plane to the runway so it won't burn."

"Worth a try. Let's go!"

Crawling over the dirt pile, they headed for the plane as Zeros made another pass at the line of planes. Bullets ripped the fuselage and wings of the Colonel's B-17, and the men hit the ground just as a tire exploded. Once more they raced through the waist-high grass, reached the airplane, opened the access door and swung up inside. Dick started the outside engine on the right but failed to get the engine on the left to turn over. He released the brake and pushed the throttle forward, hoping one engine could move the big plane. The big ship vibrated and shuddered, but would only pivot about the flat tire. Realizing the aircraft was full of aviation gasoline and still under attack, he shut down the engine and found the exit hatch.

The two men dropped out of the plane, zigzagging back to the foxhole and leapt in. The fire was now approaching the foxhole with smoke so thick they could not breathe and the heat was unbearable. They crawled out, dashing through the fire line to another foxhole two hundred feet away, while dodging bullets from the fighters. When they reached the excavation they discovered Tony had a bullet hole through the first aid packet on his belt.

Many of the men rushing out of the mess hall sought refuge in a ditch along the road, only to become perfect targets for the strafing Zeros who made repeated passes at the huddled men.

Cries of agony soon filled the air, drowned out by the swarming fighter planes and the noise of the grass fire. Airmen crawled into trucks and jeeps trying to escape, only to be prime targets for the air invaders.

In the period of one half-hour, the Japanese attack force had successfully decimated most of the buildings at Clark Field. They had destroyed thirty bombers and severely crippled five more. The fighter squadron no longer existed. Had any maintenance facilities been spared, several damaged P-40s might have been rebuilt to make two or three whole planes in a few days, but all service buildings were demolished.

The attacking planes left the battle site as quickly as they had arrived. The stunned men slowly crawled out of their hiding places, assessing the damage and responding to the cries of the wounded men. Trucks that still worked became ambulances, and the few lightly damaged buildings cleaned to be used as hospitals.

Building fires ultimately burned out, but the thick coogan grass burned throughout the night. The Base Commander directed remaining officers to take charge to organize recovery activities.

Dick Lang, 19th Bombardment Group, joined a group of men who would spend the rest of the day assisting with the wounded, carting them to the infirmary. His crew used one of the operable flat trucks, making numerous trips about the field the remainder of the day collecting the human body parts that littered the base. From foxholes, they recovered charred bodies of soldiers who did not escape the intense smoke from the grass fire.

One crew worked on the power plant, in an attempt to have electricity available the next day. Many of the soldiers just ambled about—sweaty, dirty, and stunned.

A mess line was hurriedly set up in the open to feed the men as they went about their tasks. Lang was too nauseated to eat, but filled his canteen with water to offset dehydration from the oppressive heat.

As darkness fell, the exhausted men retrieved blankets from the damaged supply room. Lang and members of his crew joined other soldiers as they headed to a banana grove some distance from the field. They were far enough from the field to avoid exposure to additional bombing, should the Japanese return. The men wrapped in blankets and stretched out on the ground for an exhausted sleep.

At one end of the runway, the lone partially concealed B-17 with no engines was the only undamaged airplane on the base. It did have one small hole in the fuselage made by a staff officer who tried to hit a Zero with a .45 Colt automatic pistol.

War had come to the Philippine Islands and the United States of America.

Chapter Two

PASSAGE TO MINDANAO

Sleeping on the uneven slope was most uncomfortable. Lang's six foot three body did not fit the standard GI blanket, and he ached from trying to adjust to the lumpy ground. Sleeping without mosquito netting required constant movement and furtive slapping throughout the night. It would have been better to have slept in the damaged barracks. At least you were off the ground.

Their elevated barracks of wooden posts and beams with nipa palm leaves for roofing and mahogany flooring were prime targets for the Japanese. The barracks suffered several strafing runs by the attacking Zeros. The men did not want to sleep in the damaged building as they were concerned the Japanese might be back for another pass. The woven bamboo swalley walls provided privacy, but even with insect screens it was necessary to drape mosquito netting over the steel cots. At least the beds and footlockers were off the ground, safe from the heavy downpours that occurred regularly.

Lang awakened several times during the night from the noise of airplanes apparently headed for Manila. The distant explosions confirmed the Japanese were serious in continuing their air assault. Lang slept fitfully until the first light of dawn.

A food line had been hastily set up, and hot coffee helped to reposition the cobwebs in his tired mind. After breakfast the men visited their barracks, looking for any remaining personal possessions that might have survived. Most everything was full of holes:

footlockers, hanging clothes, duffel bags, shoes, everything. The mahogany flooring was a series of random splinters. They managed to put a few personal toiletries in a knapsack, and then reported for muster. Groups of men were assigned to clean up the debris, assess damage, and put things back in some semblance of order.

Each man was issued a side arm, a .45 caliber pistol and holster. It would not shoot down airplanes, but might be needed for personal defense at close quarters if the island was invaded. If an invasion should occur other weapons would be issued, as the entire air staff would be called upon to serve as infantry soldiers. Lang located a Filipino-made bolo knife, twenty-four inches long and razor sharp. It became a standard part of his uniform, and he would carry it on his equipment belt until he left the islands.

As the day progressed the airfield was visited by an occasional Mitsubishi or several Zeros that would drop a single bomb or make a strafing pass to harass the repair efforts. There were a few defensive anti-aircraft weapons stationed around the field that helped to keep their visits short. This continued for several days, but the enemy's emphasis had shifted to Manila. Word was received that the Grand Hotel in Manilla, anticipating the impending invasion, threw an enormous elegant party complete with dinner, dancing, horns and funny hats. It was an orgy to be remembered by those in attendance until the end of the war.

The B-17s that left mid-morning on December 8th remained on airfields on Mindanao. Occasionally an obsolescent B-18 would fly into Clark Field to pick up members of maintenance crews needed to service the re-located planes. Some crews were reluctant to fly in the older obsolete bombers, favoring the B-17. One B-18 arriving at Clark Field around dusk was mistaken for a Mitsubishi bomber, receiving a number of bullet holes from anxious base defenders that blew out the nose plastic. The plane, on a turnaround flight, returned to Mindanao carrying maintenance personnel. Without a nose cone in the plane, it had to be a cold, drafty flight.

Japanese assault troops landed on Luzon and Leyte on

December 10, 1941 and started their inland push. Instead of meeting the Japanese on the beach, the army deployed their American and Filipino troops in a defensive posture inland, and did their best to repel the invaders. Once the Japanese established a foothold on the beach, they proceeded inland with ferocity. Without air support there was little opportunity for the defenders to mount a counter-offensive. A number of Filipino National Guardsmen who had little training threw down their rifles, disposed of their uniforms, and disappeared into the hills.

Postwar assessments indicate General Douglas MacArthur, considered a brilliant and capable military strategist, did not understand the importance of air power to provide reconnaissance, information, or protection at that time. It was one of many apparent miscalculations in the defense of the Philippine Islands.

For two weeks, the 19th Maintenance Squadron struggled to repair the facilities at Clark Field. However, Clark Field was without airplanes, and the maintenance crews of the 19th were needed to service whatever airplanes were available, wherever they were. As the Japanese moved inland, the Filipino Army evacuated Manila, declaring it an "open city." This designation was intended to save destruction of the buildings and occupants by the invading forces, since there was no military defense within the city. Many of the ground staff and civilian personnel were in an orderly retreat toward the highly defensible Bataan peninsula. The solid rock landform projected out into Manila Bay, with the small island of Corregidor just two miles off the peninsula tip. Both Bataan and Corregidor contained an extensive cave system for defense and storage of military and food supplies, as well as concealed cannon emplacements. The covering jungle provided concealment for infantry defenses. However, it provided no cover from naval and air bombardment.

The Philippine Islands were originally formed by volcanic eruptions caused by the buckling of the earth's crust during a massive collision of two tectonic plates over fifty million years ago. The islands are the tops of mountains formed by the outpouring of molten materials from the earth's interior. Most of the islands contain mountain ranges with steep, deep valleys, covered years later by dense vegetation that decayed to form a rich porous soil that created even denser foliage. Volcanic action continues today with eleven active volcanoes distributed throughout the islands that continue to flow molten material. The geologic aberration that created the islands also created a depression off the island of Mindanao that drops seven miles into the watery depths; it is the deepest depression on the earth's surface. Approximately eighty miles wide and three hundred miles long, it parallels the eastern shore of the island of Mindanao.

The solid rock islands covered by jungle growth contained infrequent areas of plains of sea detritus and volcanic ash scattered at various locations. Over seven thousand one hundred islands comprise the Philippine archipelago. Only four hundred of the islands are inhabited, and most islands are less than one square mile in size. Coarse grass covers about eighteen percent of the landform, and forty-eight percent covered by jungle growth. The remaining percentage is tillable ground.

On Christmas Eve 1941, the 19th Bombardment Group abandoned Clark field and boarded trucks bound for the Bataan peninsula. Once on Bataan, six hundred pilots, crewmembers and maintenance staff assembled for a trip to Mindanao Island to service the aircraft located there. Two days later the men rode in the same trucks to the docks at the port of Marveilles, and boarded an ancient rusty steamer, the "Maayon", bound for Mindanao.

As Lang carried his duffel up the gangway, he considered the prospect of once again servicing airplanes. He had spent a year learning his craft, and up to this point had worked servicing a B-17 for just three hours. At least Mindanao was far enough away that the 19th BG could work on aircraft without being bothered by the Japanese.

Well after dark on December 29, the Maayon made its way out of the harbor, past Corregidor, and headed south between the islands. They chugged along through the night, and at sunrise were approaching the island of Mindoro. About mid-morning, as they skirted the northeast shore of Mindoro, a lone single-engine seaplane approached from the northwest. A navy lookout with oversized binoculars shouted, "It's an American navy plane!" Suddenly the ship rocked from a violent explosion, throwing water over the men on deck. They discovered it was not an American plane.

With no defensive artillery aboard ship, the Japanese pilot was having a great time. The plane made several runs, dropping a single bomb each time, and each time just missing his target. The seventh bomb caused a large indentation, portside amidships of the steamer, just opposite where Lang was huddled under a stack of timbers. He felt absolutely helpless with nothing to throw back at the seaplane.

Several blasts from the steam whistle gave the command to abandon ship. Land was only about a mile away and the too few lifeboats were over crowded, so Lang and several hundred men jumped overboard and started swimming for shore. A sergeant grabbed Lang's hand, shouting, "I can't swim. Help me!" When they hit the water, the sergeant began dog paddling frantically, beating nearly everyone to the beach. Another young man had saved a bottle of wine for Mindanao, and when the bombing started, uncorked it, drinking the entire bottle. When he jumped from the deck and began swimming, he started vomiting and had to be assisted to shore. Once on shore he was questioned by the airmen whether his sickness was caused by the intense exercise or the quality of the Filipino wine.

The young man who was probably the sickest of all put a small box of matches between his teeth to lessen the concussion from the bombs. When the bombing was over he reached for a cigarette, realized where the matches had gone, and became violently ill.

Once ashore, the men moved inland from the beach, hiding in the jungle—waiting for more Japanese planes to arrive. Lang found a quiet spot under a large tree fern and stretched his large frame on some dried fronds. Stretching out on his back, he put his arm over his eyes, uncomfortable in his wet clothes. After catching his breath, he mused, "What the hell am I doing here? What am I doing on this unknown island in this godforsaken jungle?"

It seemed only a few months ago in the fall of 1939 that he joined his two friends on the long drive from Marshalltown, Iowa to Riverside, California to visit a fourth friend who extolled the virtues of living in Southern California. While there, Dick decided to enlist in the medical corps, because of his favorable experience working in a Marshalltown hospital. Having spent three years in the Iowa National Guard in Marshalltown after high school meant he did not have to suffer through basic training. During his physical at March Field, they discovered a condition that put him in the base hospital for a few days. They finally accepted him for a three-year enlistment in the medical corps. Assigned to the March Field Base Hospital, he carried bedpans, moved furniture, carried bedpans, gave enemas, carried bedpans, cleaned the surgical suites, and performed duties as a glorified nurse's assistant. He loved to watch surgery, and spent his off time watching operations. He also played basketball for exercise. Growing up on a farm as a member of a large family never permitted participation in sports, but he was a strapping six foot three and naturally athletic.

During a break one afternoon while shooting baskets on an outdoor court, an officer in the Air Corps approached him to talk about basketball. He was a Special Services Officer in the Air

Corps, and it seemed Headquarters Company had a pretty good basketball team, but they needed a "big man at center." At that time six-three was tall. It necessitated transferring out of the Medical Corps to the Air Corps, but Dick decided it would be fun to play basketball in southern California. Dick took the bait and transferred to Headquarters Company of the 19th Bombardment Group. He spent several months traveling to other air bases on the west coast playing basketball and living a rather carefree life. In addition, the team played in the local Riverside League and eventually won the city championship. While playing, he attended the Curtis-Wright Technical School for Aircraft Maintenance, and in five months learned how to take apart a B-17 and put it back together. On February 21, 1941, he received his Certificate of Technical Training, completing the Airplane Mechanics Course, with a Very Satisfactory rating. The special rating was an accomplishment of which Lang has always been very proud. His grade sheet is carried in his wallet to this day.

Four months later, the Nineteenth BG went to the Philippine Islands for "six months maneuvers."

"Why the hell didn't I stay in the medical corps? I could be sitting on my butt in southern California right now!" He squirmed inside damp clothes and swung at the numerous gnats swarming overhead.

Headed for overseas, Lang boarded the Army transport "Holbrook" in San Francisco on October 4th, 1941, and landed in Manila, Philippine Islands, on October 23. The Holbrook was originally one of the "President" liners, converted to a troop ship holding two thousand men. The ship was over six hundred feet long and seemed stable enough while tied to the dock. Boarding the ship mid-afternoon, the men of the 19th BG crawled down the winding stairs and found bunks several decks below the water line. Officers had the good fortune of usually being quartered above deck. Footlockers were stored in a different hold, and the enlisted men would have to live out of a small canvas bag for three long weeks during the trip over.

An army band played military marches as tugboats pushed the

Holbrook away from the dock. The large ship rocked as the pilot boat guided it out of the harbor, through the deep-water channel, and under the Golden Gate Bridge. Passing under the bridge was exciting for the Iowa farm boy, as the new span was only four years old and one of the marvels of engineering of the twentieth century. Past the bridge they hit the rough water just outside the bay area, and the large ship responded by rolling and tossing. Within minutes two thousand airmen became seasick, some more violently than others. It was the start of a long, tedious trip. Below deck the bunks were stacked five high and spaced so tightly that in order to change sleeping positions, the two hundred thirty pound Lang had to get out of the bunk. The air was heavy and close, food passable, and seasickness unbearable. Those who did not get seasick became nauseated from the frequent messes made by the others who never quite made it to the head (toilet, in navy terms).

The first morning out men went topside to 'get some air' and would climb the steel stair/ladders several times per day just to be able to breathe. With not much to do, men read, napped, climbed the stairs, pulled KP (kitchen police, or food preparation / dishwashing duties) and in true Army tradition, complained about everything.

All the difficult living conditions were bleak, but made worse by the cold saltwater showers. Saltwater soap had the consistency of sand bricks, with little lather and less cleansing action. Bathing was infrequent, until the men learned that if they volunteered for KP, they would gain access to a hot shower. And also a full stomach.

Five days later, they neared the Hawaiian Islands and were informed they would get an eight-hour pass to go ashore. Living under close conditions, out of a small canvas bag holding few clean clothes, with few toiletries that survived saltwater, discouraged some men from even leaving the ship.

The Holbrook's trip took them via Guam, where the ship anchored for a day. The bright sunshine and the clear water were much too inviting. A number of the men leapt off the ship, dropping forty feet to the water below. When the ship's bridge announced the waters contained sharks, there was a mass exodus out of the water, with the men scrambling up a cargo net dropped for their return to the ship. Sharks were not actually seen, but their possible presence was enough to discourage everyone.

The Holbrook finally entered Manila Harbor on Luzon, Philippine Islands. Landing at the dock in Manila, the men disembarked at night, and traveling through the dimly-lit city was a most welcome change from the rusty ship. They boarded busses resembling school busses, and taken inland forty miles up a narrow winding road surrounded by barrios and makeshift buildings. The busses climbed over one hundred feet up to a rolling plain, to Clark Field adjacent to Fort Stotsenburg, in Pampanga Province. They moved into crude but neat barracks set up off the ground, with mahogany floors, swalley walls (woven bamboo) and thatched roofs made of nipa palm fronds. There were electric lights, and most important, hot, fresh water.

A whistle jolted Lang back to reality. He sat up and looked around at the jungle plants and the men scattered about. "Why the hell did I leave California? I could be sleeping between white sheets. I could even smell good once and awhile!"

When it was apparent there were no additional Japanese planes in the area, the officers called the troops back to the beach where lifeboats ferried the men back to the steamer. The Maayon once again got underway. For the rest of the trip there were no more air raids, or brushes with disaster.

The Maayon arrived at the port of Cagayan, in Macajalar Bay, Mindanao, early on the morning of January 1, 1942.

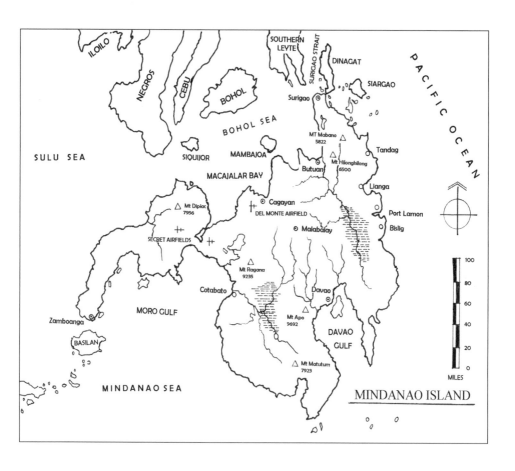

ILOILO

NEGROS

CEBU

BOHOL

SOUTHERN
LEVTE

SURIGAO STRAIT

DINAGAT

SIARGAO

PACIFIC OCEAN

Surigao

BOHOL SEA

MT Mabano
5822

Tandag

SULU SEA

SIQUIJOR

MAMBAJOA

MACAJALAR BAY

Butuan

Mt Hilonghilong
6500

Lianga

Cagayan
DEL MONTE AIRFIELD

Port Lamon

△ Mt Dipiac
7956

Bislig

SECRET AIRFIELDS

Malabalay

△ Mt Ragana
9235

Cotabato

Davao

MORO GULF

Mt Apo
9692

Zamboanga

DAVAO
GULF

BASILAN

△ Mt Matutum
7923

MINDANAO SEA

MINDANAO ISLAND

100

80

60

40

20

0

MILES

Chapter Three

SURRENDER

The soldiers disembarked from the Maayon and immediately boarded busses headed inland. Traveling through the barrios, or small villages, the busses finally followed a winding jungle road climbing several hundred feet to a large plateau where there was a pineapple plantation. The Del Monte Company owned eighteen thousand acres of rolling land—one of the largest plains areas devoted to raising pineapples in the Philippines. The plantation produced rich succulent pineapples and contained a large processing plant for canning them. The plantation was surrounded by the barrios of people who worked in the fields and canning factories. Nearby was a grass runway airstrip surrounded by several B-17 and B-18 bombers, once again neatly lined up with military precision.

The new arrivals were told to find housing in some of the two-man tents scattered about in coogan grass surrounding the airfield. Earlier arrivals of the 19th BG had been servicing the airplanes with what few tools and spare parts they could find. The new arrivals first found the mess tent, had a midnight snack, and began searching in the dark for a vacant tent to spend the night.

The Japanese army invaded Mindoro and Leyte, and were working their way south as additional supplies and troops arrived from Japan. In a week or two, they would invade northern Mindanao, a few days later land on western Mindanao and finally southern Mindanao. Their intent was not to inhabit the entire island (that is roughly the size of the state of Indiana but configured much differently) but to control the main ports in larger coastal cities in order to patrol the coasts with motor launches.

At this same time, the aggressive and well-planned Japanese expansion continued in the southwest Pacific. Simultaneously, Burma, Java and New Guinea were invaded. After a month of fighting, by March 9th 1942, they would overrun Java, Burma's capitol Rangoon, and Singapore.

Conditions in Bataan and Corregidor were equally as bleak. The 19th BG was fortunate to leave the island when they did. As the American/Filipino Army fought a "brilliant defensive maneuver," they left behind food supplies to feed one hundred thousand people for five months, a costly error. Retreating to the Bataan peninsula without protective American air cover meant they were subject to air strikes and naval bombardment by the Japanese. The sixty-five thousand civilian personnel/staff and twenty-six thousand military continued to fight a defensive war, retreating into the jungle peninsula and the extensive cave system built throughout the rocky terrain.

The supply resources available to General MacArthur were meager. The soldiers were poorly equipped and inadequately armed, and most of the Filipino home guard were inadequately trained. The soldiers fought desperately, but outmoded weapons refused to fire, equipment would not work, grenades failed to explode, and two-thirds of the mortar shells were duds.

General Douglas MacArthur directed the retreat from his beautifully appointed quarters on Corregidor Island. Since he never physically went to Bataan, disgruntled troops gave him the moniker "Dugout Doug." Instead of meeting the Japanese on the beaches and utilizing what little airpower was available to repel the invaders, the command staff chose to fight inland at strategic points. Without control of the air the resistance was spirited, but not successful. Once the defenders were confined on the peninsula, the Japanese had only to wait until disease, lack of medicine, ammunition and food forced the defenders to submit to their demands.

The General Staff in Washington DC sent a direct order for General MacArthur to leave the Philippines and move his staff to Australia. In Australia they could regroup, assess strategic needs, and mount a new offensive against the Japanese. The Navy and the Army were in heated disagreement over who should be the supreme commander in the Pacific Theater of Operations; pride and egos continued to contribute to the confusion. Navy brass felt it was a "navy war" and were not about to relinquish control of the Navy to a "land general." General Douglas MacArthur had distinguished himself as an outstanding soldier, but sometimes his "self-centered bravado" was overwhelming. It was a conflict not easily resolved.

Since General MacArthur was leaving for Australia, he transferred the command of the defense of the Philippine Islands over to General Jonathan Wainwright, in order to comply with the Washington DC directive. The defenders received numerous messages from command headquarters in Washington DC that naval and air support were on the way. However, it never arrived nor was the support ever initiated. The President directed the Chief of Staff that, with the resources at hand, the war in Europe was to receive primary attention. With the battleships lying at the bottom of Pearl Harbor, there was not enough naval power to respond to the immediate need for naval support in the Philippines. The aircraft carriers that survived by being away from Pearl Harbor during the December 7th attack could not risk exposure to the Japanese navy that was still in full force. A campaign to support the military in the Philippine Islands was redirected to Europe, and the men and women who served in the Philippine Islands were sacrificed. General Douglas MacArthur never again trusted his commander-in-chief, President Franklin Roosevelt, after this incident of duplicity.

On a pitch-black night in March 1942, General MacArthur and his wife and son, members of his military staff, members of the Philippine government, and his family's personal Filipino staff, boarded four PT boats on Corregidor and headed for Mindanao Island, 1000 miles to the south. From there, they would fly to Australia.

During the months of January and February, Pfc. Dick Lang and other members of the 19th Bomb Group began their conversion from maintenance men to ground troops. Since they were now under the control of the US Army stationed in the area, they began preparing for the defense of the island. A few bombers continued to fly in and out of the Del Monte airport, but most planes were distributed to airfields concealed in the jungle.

Several older and obsolete B-18s, the two engine bubble-nosed bombers, still remained at Del Monte field, kept in top shape by the maintenance crews; that is until one day a Japanese Zero flew over, dropped two bombs, and decommissioned all airplanes. The grass runway was repaired so incoming flights could continue to land and take off.

On March 15th Lang and seven other airmen were ordered to report for special duty at the airfield. The eight-man detail reported to assist loading four B-17 bombers that were under a good deal of security. The men drove two loaded trucks to the airfield, backed them up to the B-17, and transferred the contents to the airplane. A fleet of autos arrived, and the passengers got out of the cars. The soldiers were surprised to learn these planes were to take General MacArthur and his staff to Australia. The general was in full uniform, complete with campaign ribbons, and wore his famous cap with "scrambled eggs" on the visor. The men loaded the boxes, bags and baggage of those leaving the island. Accompanying the General were his wife, young son, and several servants. There were also numerous cases of the sweet Del Monte canned pineapple and several pieces of personal furniture.

The planes were finally loaded and the loading detail was standing by when the pilots arrived. The pilot of the general's plane, a young Lieutenant named Adams, did a thorough preflight inspection. After checking inside his airplane, he immediately issued an ultimatum. "The plane is too overloaded to get off of the ground. Get that damned stuff out of the plane or I won't fly it!" The Colonels and staff members were shocked that this young officer would be so blunt with the ranking officers and the Commanding General of the Pacific Army.

Two 6 x 6 trucks were backed up to the airplane and Lang and the crew proceeded to unload the furniture, as well as all the cases of canned pineapple; juice, chunks, and sliced rings. Meanwhile, the General stood stern and red-faced, puffing on his corncob pipe —frustrated but quiet. Once the excess baggage was unloaded, the pilot said firmly, "Get everyone on board and let's get out of here." The General, his wife, son, and Filipino staff, about ten in number, boarded Lt. Adams plane. As the General mounted the top step, he set his jaw and looked back, striking a dramatic pose. He forcefully announced to the officers and soldiers in attendance, and to the people of the Philippine Islands, "I - shall - return!"

The remaining military staff and Filipino government officials entered the other planes, about thirty or forty persons per plane. They each had only their briefcase and a small satchel of clothes. The four planes taxied down the rolling plains of the field, turned and roared down the runway one by one, taking off over the bluffs, over the ocean, headed for Australia.

The loading detail returned to their regular duties, training to defend the island.

The canned pineapple removed from the plane found its way to the mess hall. The soldiers thoroughly enjoyed it, almost as much as the story of Lieutenant Adams' taking firm control of his airplane in the face of senior military officers.

The soldiers received word that conditions on Bataan were very severe, and several trips were made from Mindanao to deliver medicine and supplies with PT boats and the one remaining B-18. Lang did not make any trips to the endangered peninsula, but helped to round up what few medical supplies could be located. Conditions continued to deteriorate. The defenders of Bataan ran out of food, ran low on ammunition, and most troops suffered from malnutrition, malaria and dysentery. Finally, General Wainwright recognized the futility of his position and capitulated to the Japanese forces. Unknown to the General, the Japanese were also suffering from disease, dengue fever, malaria and jungle fever. After the war it was discovered that a concentrated offensive effort might have overturned the war situation on Luzon, but there was neither the firepower nor physical energy to retaliate.

With the surrender, the Japanese took control of over a hundred thousand US and Filipino soldiers and personnel. Most of the prisoners were staff and government personnel, not trained soldiers. All of them were forced to march to a prison camp located sixty miles away, which became the infamous "Bataan Death March," where Americans and Filipinos first experienced the brutality and inhumanity of the soldiers of Japan.

A few days after the fall of Bataan, Japanese forces landed on northern Mindanao. American and Filipino soldiers, including Lang, met them at the beach. Armed with rifles and several machine guns, the soldiers positioned themselves for maximum firepower from the hills above the landing area. The Japanese took heavy losses in establishing a beachhead, but the air cover and naval support ultimately drove the defenders from the low hills back into the jungle. Ten days later, the American and Filipino soldiers were confronted by the decision to surrender.

On April 9, 1942, fighting finally ended on Bataan and on May 6 Corregidor fell to the Japanese. On May 3, some members of General Wainwright's staff and a few army nurses managed to escape by submarine from Corregidor and found their way to Australia. They were the last group to get off the island before the formal surrender.

The terms and conditions of surrender were difficult to negotiate. General Wainwright was prepared to surrender Bataan and its environs. However, the Japanese General refused to accept the surrender unless the armies of the entire Philippine Islands capitulated. Without knowing the status of the conflict on other islands, General Wainwright, with over one hundred thousand sick and malnourished troops, and without any bargaining position whatsoever, finally agreed to surrender all of the islands in the Philippines.

When news of the surrender reached Mindanao, the commanding US Army Colonel called the troops together. He informed the men that all soldiers of the US Army would lay down their arms and surrender to the Japanese. The names of soldiers who did not comply were to be kept in military files, and when the war was over those men would be dishonorably discharged for not following a direct order. It was a threat the men who fought at the Japanese landing at Cagayan did not appreciate. Having defended the beach during the Japanese landings, a number of men were adamant about not surrendering.

Lang's squad spent the day on a special detail away from the main base, which gave them an opportunity to consider the perils of becoming a prisoner of war. Lang's training with the National Guard created a mindset that he would rather fight than become a prisoner. After considerable discussion, the group decided to take their chances in the hills rather than a prison camp. Rumors of brutality and atrocities committed by the Japanese on Bataan were not lost on these men.

One of the non-coms worked in the motor pool and managed to hide a four-door 1938 Buick staff car in a secluded area on the base in a semi-jungle area, anticipating a hasty departure. The men collected ammunition, guns and some food staples and hid them in the car.

When the formation ordering the surrender was dismissed, six men including two officers and Dick Lang, returned to their tents to select what they would take with them in their packs. Gathering their personal effects, they crept to the car filled with weapons, ammunition, and all the food they could get in the car. Dick drove the car on the rough dirt road to Malaybalay, about fifty miles away.

In Malaybalay, they met six of their compatriots who arrived later. Negotiating with local natives, the men purchased three carabaos, a relative of the water buffalo, to pack their equipment into the jungle. They would also serve as a food source if things got desperate. Loading the supplies on the backs of the three carabaos, they would travel as far as they could on jungle trails until they would have to continue on foot, carrying their supplies.

Without reporting in, defying the direct order, the men headed inland on a jungle trail where they probably would not encounter any Japanese. Officially, they were absent without leave (AWOL) from the United States Army, subject to court-martial. They entered a new phase of their military life that would last over two years, take them to many different areas on Mindanao Island and place them in a number of ominous personal challenges.

It was their intent to work their way to the east coast of Mindanao and commandeer a boat to take them to Australia.

First, they had to get to the coast. The group started east out of Malaybalay. From there to the coast was nothing but jungle.

Chapter Four

INTO THE JUNGLE

"I don't know if going into the jungle is such a good idea!"

"Ain't no way I'm gonna volunteer to be a prisoner of the Japs."

"Just so we don't meet any hostiles in the hills. Some of the insurgents can be downright nasty. They don't like Americans, Christians, or city folks."

"Get going you lazy beast. You are the slowest animal I've ever seen." Lang rapped the carabao across the rump with his bamboo walking stick, but the animal ignored him and continued to amble along at its own pace. "I'm naming you "snafu." You are the slowest sumbitch in the islands!"

The men hiked southeast through a plain area covered with coogan grass, sometimes called cogon grass, which varied from three feet to eight feet in height. They skirted the town of Malaybalay and started up into the foothills, into the dense jungle. They stopped only briefly to snatch a bit of food before continuing. Once in the jungle, they followed a trail that ascended slowly up the mountainside that was interspersed with deep gullies. They continued to travel for three days, day and night, before stopping to rest.

Mindanao topography consists of sharply rising hills, which branch out from the mountains. The second tallest mountain on the island, Ragang, reached over 9,200 feet, and the volcano Apo close to the eastern shore of the island near Davao, rises out of the bay 9,690 feet. Mt. Apo is one of the eleven volcanoes still active in the islands. Mt. Matutum at the southern tip tops out at 7,520 feet. Connecting ridges and dramatic valleys make the terrain all but impossible for any vehicular roads as well as difficult for footpaths, with constant steep rises and descents.

The mountain trails wander as though there is no reason to stop and at times are so grown over with plant life it is almost like cutting a new trail. Trails are slippery and difficult because they never dry out. Rainfall, depending on the side of the island and prevailing winds, varies from forty inches to two hundred inches per year. Since the island is mostly rock covered by an interlocking root system that does not absorb water, intense rainfall creates rushing water that will cause chaos in a ravine in a very short time. Crossing a gully full of rushing water is dangerous since the depth of the gully cannot be gauged without probing.

The jungle cover of the islands reflects the uniqueness of the area. Several thousand years of plant life leave intertwining roots, some decaying to make a rich but thin soil base. The warm climate with uniform temperatures of seventy to ninety degrees not only encourages growth of flora, but also microorganisms that are hostile to humans. Trails grow over in a very short time and must be re-widened to remain passable in most instances. The jungle consists of ground plants, under-story bushes and shrubs, and tall trees that sprout above the under-story cover. Mature trees may be over one hundred fifty feet tall, with a trunk diameter of over four feet. The ferns and vines, coarse grasses and decaying trees make the jungle almost impassable. A slip on the trail, grabbing a vine for support, might expose a hand to small thorns that would fester and burn or cause an instant itchy rash. All plants were suspect, particularly to the neophyte jungle soldiers.

Occasionally the jungle was dotted with wild orchids, parasitic plants that added spots of intense color to the dark greens. Filipinos named some of the nine hundred varieties of orchids with descriptive terms, such as the spider orchid, butterfly orchid, or lizard orchid. There were a wide variety of flowering bushes such as the bougainvillaea, cadena de amor, and the national flower, sampaguita, with its delicate white flower. The young soldiers who focused on avoiding capture by the Japanese ignored the beautiful flowers of the jungle. They were more intent on avoiding plants that could cut, stab and raise welts with an accidental touching.

The soldiers were occasionally startled by the white crested cockatoo bird that would scream until it "was almost purple" when frightened. It always took them by surprise, and the soldiers felt that it might alert any human inhabitants of visitors in their neighborhood. They soon learned to listen to the jungle sounds and its special language.

After moving continuously for three days the men found a flat area that could be adapted as a campground, built a fire, and settled in for two days of rest. They prepared some of their food, unrolled their bedroll and stretched out for a good night's sleep. The men were suddenly awakened by the kalow birds, with their raucous call, "kalow-kalow, kawlaw-kalaw." One bird would start the song, and thousands of birds in the area would join in a deafening intensity, and then as if on cue, abruptly stop. The silence was eerie. Once again insect sounds prevailed, with owls hooting in the background. The kalow repeated their screaming ritual every twenty minutes until the break of dawn. At first light the bojong bird that sounded like a barking dog would echo through the jungle. After the first few kalow performances, the soldiers finally succumbed to their complete exhaustion with restless but deep sleep.

Since the trail was now very difficult for the carabao to traverse, the men decided to turn loose two animals and kill one for food. Lang volunteered "snafu" to be butchered. He was happy to shoot "that &$##@& independent beast." The men dressed the animal and cut the meat in strips. They constructed a rack of branches, and hung the meat so it would dry like jerky, preserving it for eating later during their travels. The next day they repacked their provisions, since they would now be backpacking their supplies. Without a ranking military leader, the men talked out their plans and cooperated in their decisions without dissent. The men rested another day, packing and repacking their supplies, trying to determine what was most important for survival. Consideration for fighting the Japanese was secondary to surviving the jungle, rain, hunger and disease.

The jungle was foreboding, intriguing, peaceful, and frightening all at the same time. Where there was dense over-story, the penetrating light had an almost church-like quality of quiet softness. In areas where large trees had succumbed to age and degeneration, falling to the ground created a strong shaft of sunlight that echoed through the small plant life. The individual plants fought for the sustenance that would permit growth, rearranging itself in grotesque shapes, until once again the vacated over-story was solidly blocking the sun. Leaves of every configuration stretched its growth to maximum capacity using what mineral and food it could extract from the detritus that clutched its roots.

The following day as the early morning shafts of light penetrated the jungle, the men adjusted their packs, picked up their weapons and continued on the jungle trail headed in the general direction of the east coast. The trail consisted of sharp rises and steep descents, with small streams in between. They forded one river, scouting for the shallowest crossing in order to keep their packs dry. An occasional cigarette break or food snack was their only stop. When it got dark the men dropped along the trail. The only waterproof item they carried was a shelter-half. Two oil-treated canvas shapes designed by the army were fastened together to form a small two-man tent with no bottom canvas. Only one shelter-half attached to a tree made an impromptu lean-to that would keep most of the rain off of them for a short time.

When it was not raining the jungle not only dripped constantly from residual water on the leaves, but also from "cistern plants" that held water in curled leafs and built-in vessels. The "cistern plants" also provided breeding grounds for the numerous species of water-larval insects. Mosquitoes were a problem day and night. Leeches that clung to the underside of leaves would attach to any animal that brushed against the bush. One had to be constantly on the lookout for plant life causing irritation, itching and skin cuts, such as clusters of Spanish dagger with sharp points, or kunai grass with its razor sharp serrated edges.

The men continued on the trail for two more days, taking turns with a bolo knife to widen the trail as they moved along. The temperature was in the eighties, and the humidity approached one hundred percent. The effort involved in walking increased the incidence of sweating, and their wet clothing rarely dried out.

At the start of the next day the two officers, Holmes and Taylor, suffered with feet that were so skinned-up and blistered they decided to rest and heal for a day or two. After discussing the options, eight of the men decided to continue to the east coast where they would try to locate transportation to take the twelve of them to Australia. Lang and Tom Baxter decided to stay behind with the wounded, to assist them on their way when they felt better. After consulting their maps to decide upon a meeting place on the coast, the eight men packed their gear and left camp.

After waiting for a day, the officers with blistered feet decided they could not start walking for at least several more days. Again, the men consulted their maps, estimating the number of days it would take to reach the coast. It was obvious they would run out of food before they got there. Lang and Baxter decided to head out to the coast and meet the other members of their team, and volunteered to leave most of their food with the two remaining foot-sore soldiers. Two men traveling might make better time than the whole pack, and once the foot-sore soldiers felt better, they could follow at their own pace. They verified their meeting place on the coast, hoisted their packs and once more Lang and Baxter followed the path through the jungle.

Dick and Tom were making good time until two days before they entered the Agusan River Valley, an inhabited valley where they knew they could find food. They ate their last meal, certain they could replenish their supply when they reached the valley.

Unfortunately, they proceeded to get lost in a dense canyon of undergrowth. It began to rain so hard they could not see the trail. Streams were suddenly waist deep, but they kept wading, climbing, sliding, and "plugging along." Fortunately, Lang had a compass, and they started hiking straight east, hacking a new path with their bolo knives.

At nightfall they could not sleep, but shared their one shelter-half stretched over a tree branch, huddling together to avoid the hard rain. As the rain drained their body heat, they both started to shiver uncontrollably. It was impossible to stop the convulsions.

Lang, having lived in Iowa, had been exposed to temperatures well below minus twenty degrees, but never experienced reaction to cold like this. The two men sat shaking for several hours, unable to control their discomfort. They remained there for two nights suffering through the intense rain. Building a fire was out of the question as all combustible materials were thoroughly soaked. The prospect of something to eat caused some abatement in the trembling and when the rain momentarily subsided they spotted a young palm tree where they could reach the top to harvest "obud," the new growth that was edible.

They soon learned one of the laws of living in the jungle; to survive, "eat what the monkeys eat." The obud relieved the hunger pangs, but the pulpy apple-sized sprout did not furnish much nourishment. They tried to eat wild bananas, but soon learned that of the sixty or so different kinds of banana trees only four or five varieties were edible. Again, they watched what the monkeys ate.

Walking through the wet plant materials, and with the constant rain, Lang's army high-top shoes finally rotted out and were no longer wearable. This meant he would have to walk barefoot until some sort of replacement could be found.

The next morning they resumed their trek due east, hacking their way through the underbrush. Their energy level was very low, but they continued to extend themselves, alternating the lead. Lang limped along, feeling every vine and rock on his tender feet. Tree thorns required that he stop every so often to extract the small penetrations. He could avoid the big thorns, but the small ones caused just as much damage. It was on one of the thorn stops that he discovered leeches attached to his legs. The bloodsuckers, if not removed immediately, would cause open sores, that would soon become infected and ulcerated. He had to stop every ten minutes to remove ten or fifteen small leeches before they could attach too firmly.

On the evening of the second day, they came upon a lake, several miles long and about a half-mile wide. As darkness approached, they looked for high ground, at least with no standing water, where they would be dry for the night. In the morning, they could build a raft out of bamboo to cross the lake. As they were cleaning an area to sleep they smelled smoke, and noticed smoke on the horizon across the lake. It meant someone was living on the other side of the lake.

Lang drew his .45 and fired two shots in the air, hoping to get someone's attention. There was no response, so the men continued to prepare a sleeping bed for their first dry night's sleep in five days. The noise of lapping water caught their attention, and suddenly two young boys appeared on a raft, poling their way onto shore. Dick and Tom were so happy to see another individual they shouted and hugged the boys in an expression of relief and joy.

Loading their gear aboard the raft, the boys pushed the raft across the shallow lake to a landing opposite a small island. The boys then led them to a small hut, inland about two hundred feet, where they were greeted by a young Filipino couple. The young man and wife welcomed them into their house, and much to Tom and Dick's surprise, spoke English.

There was much to talk about, but the two soldiers were so exhausted they had to rest. The young wife immediately produced some boiled corn and large snails cooked on a stick, which the men devoured with the worst of table manners. The young couple gave them woven floor mats to sleep on. The men could only mutter, "Thank you. Goodnight!" before they entered a deep, welcome sleep.

The men slept until mid morning, when again the wife produced more hard roasted corn, shellfish and kalibo. Kalibo is an eighteen-inch long flat banana, cut into slices and cooked in coconut oil. It was their first hot food in over a week, and remains in Lang's memory as one of the most satisfying meals he has ever eaten.

The experience also exposed the two soldiers to the generosity and caring of the Filipino people, qualities experienced throughout their years on the islands with few exceptions.

The Philippine Islands were under the rule of Spain for over four hundred years, until they were "purchased" by the United States. The U.S. promised full and independent freedom to the people of the islands, and as a result, the islanders loved and respected the Americans. Except for one or two renegade bands of American soldiers who roamed the islands, most citizens extended friendship to the American guerrillas beyond their resources.

The soldier's clothing dried overnight, and putting on dry stockings and shirts was a decided luxury, not experienced the last few weeks. The prospect of finding new shoes was a possibility, but finding a pair of 13EE shoes in all of the Philippine Islands was a pipe dream. Since the average Filipino was about five feet tall, feet were correspondingly small. Lang would have to do the best he could to toughen the soles of his large feet.

The next morning the two soldiers were escorted to a small town a few miles away, where they made inquiries about the trail ahead. Here they learned they could get a small boat and float down the river for a few days. In the Agusan Valley, food would be more readily available and it would not be necessary to carry as much. The Filipinos in the village were most friendly and quite impressed by the tall Iowan, who stood fifteen inches taller than members of the barrio. The natives helped to find a baroto, a small dugout canoe with an outrigger, and gave the soldiers directions for locating help as they floated down the stream toward the Agusan River.

Pushing off from the riverbank, the soldiers shouted "Salamat po! Salamat po!" (Thank you! Thank you!), waved to the friendly Filipinos, and started floating down stream. It was such a relief not to have to walk and experience the agony of proceeding barefoot through the jungle. They would stop along the bank twice a day to eat corn porridge. Instead of finding food along the way, they discovered a typhoon had passed through the area two weeks earlier and ruined all the crops and food sources.

Both Tom and Dick had lost a lot of weight from their ordeal. Traveling on the river was much easier physically, but the mosquitoes were unbearable. Without mosquito nets, the nights were essentially sleepless.

Reaching the Agusan River, they scouted around to see if any Japanese had arrived in the area. Seeing none, they crossed the river, looking for a tributary that would take them closer to the east coast of Mindanao. Checking their map, they were encouraged to find they were only four or five days from the coast.

Starting up the smaller river, they had to work hard since they were going upstream on a fairly fast flowing river. Suddenly, managing the baroto was work, and it sapped all their energy, as they had to paddle constantly. Late afternoon they stopped for a long rest, and decided to spend the night. Their energy level was approaching zero, and they needed a good sleep. Up early the next morning, they fought the current for several hours before stopping to eat. They were so exhausted they could not get out of the boat to prepare their corn porridge. They munched dry corn meal, and once again entered the current, fighting to advance the small craft. Any small variance from dead ahead meant a struggle to keep their baroto upright, let alone moving forward. Lang felt nauseated and touched his forehead. He was running a temperature, but was working too hard to notice. Tom admitted he had been running one since he woke up. They realized they were in no condition to continue, and agreed to stop at the first opportunity. A few minutes later they came upon a barrio next to the riverbank, pulled their borato on the bank and collapsed. The villagers were most accommodating, waded out to beach the boat, then helped them up the riverbank.

A local townsman, Judge Malver, his wife and three children, approached and invited the men to join them at their house. Lang was so weak and exhausted he had to be carried to the house. The family had two beds and promptly put Baxter in one and Lang in the other. The family then proceeded to nurse both soldiers back to health.

Judge Malver had been a court judge in Manila, a city he loved. Often called "the Jewel of the East," Manila was named after the white mangrove flower, famous for its delicate beauty. When the Americans retreated from the city during the Japanese invasion they declared it an "open city," vacating it so it would not be destroyed. When the Japanese bombed Manila during the invasion, the Judge packed a few goods and left his beautiful home with his family for the security of the interior. Here, they intended to live out the war until the Americans returned. It was a difficult life, but the family adapted very well.

Lang's weight had dropped from two hundred twenty-five pounds to around one hundred sixty pounds. Baxter's weight loss was similar. The lack of food and the poor diet had taken their toll. The men would enjoy a two-week stay with the Judge and his family who took excellent care of them. The Malvers kept them well fed with a variety of home grown vegetables, fruits, and deer meat to replenish and balance their diet. Mrs. Malver had a small supply of wheat flour and made bread for them. The Malvers owned two female carabaos that furnished milk for the family. As a result,

Dick and Tom were served fresh milk every day, which contributed significantly to their recovery. Once again, Lang learned to appreciate the generosity and friendliness of the Philippine people. Once more, the Filipinos were more than generous.

The men stayed in bed for two weeks. One day a Japanese patrol passed near the barrio. If the two American soldiers confined to bed had been discovered by the Japanese, they would have had to shoot it out from their beds with their .45s. However, the Japanese patrol was unaware of the visiting Americans, and moved on down the trail.

At the end of two weeks the men were up and moving about. One afternoon the men were sitting in the yard talking to Judge Malver, when four American soldiers approached them. One soldier, Charlie Martin, was an American prospector who had spent considerable time scouting the islands for minerals, and was the leader of the other three men. The four were traveling to the east coast of Mindanao, providing there were no Japanese in the vicinity. Martin invited Baxter and Lang to join them. Dick realized it

was an opportunity to travel in a group with persons better prepared to live in the jungle. It seemed like a good arrangement
since the men had recovered enough to accompany them. Charlie's
group had a limited amount of canned food with them, and they
divided it among the six men. They anticipated finding enough
additional native food en route to meet their needs.

Saying farewell to Judge and Mrs. Malver and their three children was difficult. The Malver family had literally saved Dick's
and Tom's lives. Had the barrio not been friendly they would have
been left to the elements and there was not much fight left in the
two men. If one native, for fear of jeopardizing the barrio, reported
the men to a passing Japanese patrol, the patrol would have
tracked down and killed the two American soldiers and probably
the Malvers. Lang still reflects on the generosity of the Malver
family with great affection.

On July 1, 1942, Baxter and Lang joined Charlie Martin's group,
gathered their belongings and once more headed into the jungle
bound for the east coast of Mindanao.

Chapter Five

BECOMING A GUERRILLA

The six men followed the rough jungle trail for several days. When they were within one day of the coast they decided to settle in and rest before going ahead to scout for the Japanese. Scouting the territory, they managed to locate a small bamboo house with palm frond roof that would accommodate all six of them. The house contained beds, but no mattresses or sheets. The good news was they were sleeping above the ground and had mosquito netting, a luxury after nights spent on the jungle mat. Flooring was made of strips from thick bamboo spaced one-quarter inch apart, which not only permitted air to circulate, but made sweeping with a palm husk broom very easy. Privacy was again obtained with swalley interior and exterior walls. Food was readily available, and they learned what grasses and plants were edible as salad to balance their diet. They found fruit trees of jackfruit, star apple and kalamasi. They remained for a week, resting from their arduous jungle trek.

After discussing their situation, Charlie, Dick, and Tom went to the coast to assess the locale, number of Japanese troops, and the availability of a seaworthy boat. They entered a town on the coast called Lianga and talked to local citizens about location and quantity of Japanese troops. It turned out that a Japanese patrol of thirty men had passed through town just three days earlier. The Japanese occupied major cities and then sent patrols by boat and land to search the surrounding areas. Generally they did not usually bother the local citizens, but occasionally would act forcefully and brutally to keep the citizens in a state of fear of reprisal if they did not cooperate.

The Japanese practiced and lived "bushida," which literally means "death before dishonor." Buddhism was adopted as the official national religion of Japan in 1616, and to ensure acceptance, two hundred eighty thousand Japanese Christians were hunted down and killed. Honor and "saving face" became foremost in Japanese life and influenced their every action. In the military the officers physically beat non-commissioned officers to build strength and honor. The non-commissioned officers physically beat the privates to instill fear and determination. The privates became a surly lot, treating civilians and conquests as captives, with total disregard for human rights or human life. The atrocities they committed were unfathomable to the western mind. The soldiers and citizens who surrendered on Bataan were not considered "prisoners of war" according to the Geneva Convention, but were treated by the Japanese as "captives" who had no honor because "they had surrendered and lost face." "Captives" were abused to any degree their captors saw fit. The fact that the prisoners were malnourished, exhausted, and sick made them even more disgusting in the Japanese soldiers' eyes, and invited torment and atrocity. Unable to fight back, many fine individuals lost their lives due to senseless brutality. The Japanese followed procedures hoping enough prisoners would die to reduce the quantity of food and medicine they would have to supply, and did everything inhumanely possible to effectuate the reduction of numbers. Survivors reported after the war that over two hundred prisoners died every day from malnutrition, sickness, dysentery, dehydration, and physical abuse over a three-month span.

The Japanese took great pride in the fact they had not lost a military battle in over two thousand years. They believed you "win first, fight later." When they wanted territory or raw material for their industry, they would assess the situation, and attack without notice, overpowering the opponent who had no time to prepare to repulse the attack. "Win beforehand. Use a surprise attack when they are unsuspecting," was their motto. It permitted them to attack the many areas in the southwest Pacific that saw victory after victory in Java, Borneo, the Marshall Islands and the Philippines. The attack on Pearl Harbor was a continuation of a policy in use for over two thousand years. The Japanese military assumed the American people were intrinsically weak and would not fight back if they lost their navy at Pearl Harbor. History shows they would live to regret this miscalculation.

Occasionally there was a slip in the bushida code. The original commander in charge of the occupation of the Philippine Islands was Lt. Gen. Shigenor Kuroda. Once he achieved this high status he was corrupted by the soft life as conqueror of Manila. He discovered golf, and played it every day at the Manila Country Club. The general spent his evenings with geishas, specially delivered from Japan. One of the younger dedicated officers reported his activities to higher authorities, and the Lieutenant General was shipped home in disgrace. His replacement, General Yamashita, was given the responsibility to occupy and control the Philippines through tough and decisive action. Up to this point, there was not much local resistance.

When the Japanese first invaded the Philippine Islands they exhibited ferocity and unreasonable cruelty. The Filipinos lived in a fractional society with a few jungle gangs and religious Moros on the loose. The local natives disliked the native gangs who periodically assaulted them, but both parties soon developed a special hatred for the Japanese. Ultimately the disparate elements joined the citizens and resisted the foreign occupation of their homeland.

Later during the occupation, the Japanese attempted to be friendly with the local citizens. The Filipinos accepted the occasional visits by squads of Japanese and did not resist, knowing that openly showing resistance would bring beatings, family killings, or bayoneting of everyone in the area. Still later, the Japanese tried to force the Filipinos to "like" them, which united the local citizens against the Japanese even more.

The three Americans arrived in Lianga and circulated very carefully, since they did not want to have the inhabitants compromised for concealing them. The Japanese patrols were from a large garrison of troops stationed in Surigao City, located at the northern tip of Surigao Province. It was the largest of the twelve large cities along the coast. Squads of Japanese regularly traveled up and down the coast, keeping a watchful eye on their newly conquered territory, scouting for food, and observing anything suspicious.

Near Lianga the three Americans met an American mestizo (Spanish for half-breed) by the name of Mr. Goode. He was of American-Filipino mixture, and his wife was German-Filipino. A resident of the area for some time, Goode had secreted a radio receiver in the nearby hills. He invited the men to a small house well concealed in the jungle where the men could hear news broadcast from San Francisco.

It was the first news from the outside world they had heard since leaving Clark Field. England was receiving heavy bombing and the Germans were driving toward Stalingrad. News in the Pacific was not good. The Japanese had captured the Dutch East Indies, and Singapore, and American losses were high in the battle of the Java Sea. Wake Island, Guam, and Hong Kong were in Japanese hands. Just having contact with the U.S. and hearing American music was exciting for the soldiers who had spent the previous year adapting to their isolation.

Lang learned that the two officers left in the mountain jungles with blistered feet had arrived on the coast. Baxter and Lang searched the area, finally locating them, and the four shared their experiences. The two officers had hooked up with three other Americans, Captain Martin and his wife, and Lieutenant Tom Jurica. These Americans had been associated with the Luzon Stevedoring Company before the war. When the troops were ordered to surrender the three of them commandeered a large native banca, a motorized launch with a sail, with intent to sail to Australia. When they happened across the two officers, they invited the officers to accompany them to Australia. Securing provisions, they all went to sea, and were about forty miles underway when they ran into a chibasco, a wall of rain with high winds, that blew them back to shore on southeastern Mindanao. Discovered by a Japanese patrol, the five were captured and placed in temporary confinement. Captain Martin and his wife managed to escape, but the three officers were moved to a larger prison camp. The fate of the three officers is unknown; presumably either they were killed or taken to Japan to work as forced labor.

Charlie, Tom and Dick discussed their options at Lianga, to determine their next course of action. Tom Baxter decided to head down the coast south to a larger town, Hinatuan, to determine opportunities for escape to Australia.

Baxter made his way overland to Hinatuan where he scouted the city for a banca that was seaworthy. He moved around town rather easily, but was tracked down by a patrol of Japanese soldiers. It seems Baxter was betrayed by a "fifth columnist," a sympathizer of the Japanese who pretended to be anti-Japanese. Baxter was loaded aboard a motorized launch and taken to Surigao to a prison camp.

Lang ran into Baxter a year later and learned of his story. When captured, Baxter was severely beaten with rifle butts. He still had many ulcers on his legs and feet from their walk through the jungle, as did Lang. While being transported to Surigao, the Japanese enjoyed putting their cigarette butts out by squashing them on his ulcerated sores. They did not give him any food or water on the trip to Surigao, and when they put him in the prison, again beat him with their rifle butts. He was in the prison only two days when he escaped during the second night. He managed to find a caba-caba, a small baroto, on the beach, and paddled all night south down the coast where he found a small island with no Japanese. He then continued working south from island to island traveling at night, until he located some Americans and friendly Filipinos who took him in and sheltered him.

Charlie Martin was a mining engineer who discovered gold-bearing ore on Mindanao. Charlie was in his forties, and had spent a good deal of time inspecting the geology of the island. Lang and Martin remained on the coast for a few weeks letting their wounds heal. They had a comfortable house, and food was readily available. Charlie decided he would return to the interior to visit the gold mine, since he was in charge of the operation. The three men who traveled with Charlie decided to split up, since they were very sick with fever. Two of the men headed inland, and later died from their fever. The third soldier was too sick to travel, and continued to live with a Filipino family for several months. When radio contact was finally made with SOUWESPAC and submarines began to land with supplies, he was evacuated to the U.S.

In September 1942, Dick Lang learned there were a number of Americans near Tandag, a municipality about forty miles north of Lianga. Lang decided to travel up the coast to meet them. He arranged to borrow a small sailboat, and reached Tandag in two days. Locating the Guerrilla group, he found twelve or fifteen Americans, most of who were sick with malaria. Once again, he met Captain Martin and his wife, and Lieutenant Tom Jurica, who had set out for Australia. Most of the Americans Lang met around Tandag had also started toward Australia from Leyte when the military surrendered to the Japanese. Most all had run into storms that forced their return to land. One group in a banca capsized about five miles off shore, and the men were able to swim to safety. Fortunately, they found a friendly environment.

Rice, fish, and pork were plentiful in this area, and within a couple of months the men began to recover from their various maladies. Their sores healed and they were once again able to move about. Lang had gained back most of the weight he had lost, and his feet now had a thick sole pad for walking in the jungle.

Martin and Jurica related their sailing and prison adventures of their attempt to get to Australia in great detail. After hearing their story and assessing the odds on reaching Australia, Lang did some real soul searching. The number and location of the Japanese in the outlying islands were unknown. Far too many things could go wrong when sailing a small boat across the south Pacific. The unpredictability of the violent storms on small craft was a deterrent. The chance of not finding land would mean death by dehydration and starvation.

Lang finally made the decision to stay on Mindanao, join the guerrilla forces, and harass the Japanese until General MacArthur returned.

While in Tandag, the soldiers were visited by a young member of the local constabulary force named Earnesto Lancen. Ernie, as he was called, was an engaging young man, extremely handsome and well educated. He was a mestizo, half American and half Filipino. He spoke several Filipino dialects as well as English. Ernie was quite impressed with the tall, soft-spoken Iowan, offering his services to Lang to be his assistant. Dick Lang did not know how to respond to this young energetic man; as a private first class in the army, he was not prepared to have an assistant. He finally agreed to let Ernie accompany him on their travels, and Ernie became indispensable in later encounters with the Filipinos. He also served as a semi-houseboy, fixing Dick's coffee, finding suitable clothing and preparing food. Ernie's ability to speak several Filipino dialects later proved invaluable.

Guerrilla activities were not well organized and had not really begun on the east coast of Mindanao. Further west around Cagayan, the resistance was much better organized. Unfortunately, there were several bands of American and Filipino soldiers creating problems on the east coast. Several different groups of Filipinos were lead by self-serving ambitious leaders wanting to control territory and collect largesse from local communities. They were fiercely independent and often fought among themselves. Also there were two or three renegade bands of a few American soldiers who did not want to follow their military commanders, and became independently insolent. They raided barrios to steal enough food to last for a week, then would attack another barrio when their food was gone. Other American soldiers, who under the same circumstances wanted to work with the local Filipinos to organize a systematic resistance to the Japanese, disliked these renegades. Instead of confronting the gangs, they avoided them.

The Moros were a fiercely independent group of religious Muslims living high in the mountains that resisted the regular Philippine government and definitely did not like Christians. They were really only a problem when you entered their territory; they defended it with savage intensity.

One of the main challenges on the island was to attempt to

have these disparate groups unite in the common cause of fighting the Japanese. It was a major undertaking. Colonel Fertig, the military Commanding Officer on the island of Mindanao made a concentrated effort to unite these elements, and with special effort, his undertaking was ultimately successful.

During the long journey of the last six months, Lang's clothing had been exposed to variations of dampness, heat, and body salt, and was literally rotting away. In Tandag, Ernie managed to find a Filipino tailor who made clothing from a burlap like material to fit Lang's large frame. The Filipinos, as well as some Chinese, were very adept at sewing and did quality work. The coarse fabric was not uncomfortable. Not having ready-made underwear took some getting used to. For underwear, the Americans adopted the wearing of a cord or G-string around their waist with a simple cloth pulled through their legs, like the natives who worked in the rice paddies. It was not stylish, but beat the chafing by the coarse fabric.

Shoes were still out of the question for Lang. Attempts at making sandals were unsuccessful since they were not reliable when running, and slipped off while climbing steep, difficult trails. The pad on the bottom of Lang's feet was now tough enough to stand the exposure on most of the trails. It was his only option.

Lang, now committed to becoming a guerrilla, began scouting the area for guns, ammunition, and men willing to fight. They contacted many American and Filipino ex-soldiers who had escaped to the hills when the Philippines fell. There were few rifles, as soldiers discarded anything heavy when traveling through the jungle. Lang did manage to get a small group of volunteers together who agreed to fight the Japanese. Then the task was to train and equip them as a fighting unit. The area was so mountainous and covered with jungle, there were no roads for access. It was perfect for their rendezvous and training, even if they lacked training equipment.

In January 1943, they heard about an organization on Mindanao's north coast, somewhere in Misamis Oriental, not far from the city of Cagayan. Colonel Fertig formed a guerrilla organization at that location, and there were a number of Americans serving there. It appeared to be a ten or twelve days travel by foot and baroto from Tandag. Lang and several of the men decided to it was worth the effort to check it out. It could well be a source for equipment, rifles, and ammunition to equip the Tandag troops.

Lang, John Gain, Oscar Smith, and Frank Divine, all Americans, plus Ernie, decided to make the trip, prepared their packs and headed back into the jungle. After three days traveling, they met an American, a Mr. McCarthy, with his Filipino wife and children. McCarthy was about sixty-five years old, a long time resident who operated a sawmill before the war, but retreated into the jungle in makeshift quarters to avoid the Japanese. McCarthy had lost two sons fighting with the guerrillas. He welcomed the men to stay with his family, and the Americans stayed for two days, resting up for the hazardous trip. The local Filipinos liked and respected McCarthy and showed him every courtesy since he was for all practical purposes "one of them."

During the second day another white man arrived who happened to be a very close friend of the McCarthys. Waldo Neveling was a German citizen, a confirmed Nazi who hated the Japanese, and had joined a band of guerrillas. He was also on his way to the headquarters of the American guerrilla organization. Waldo joined the four Americans and Ernie, and early the next morning the six entered the dense jungle and mountainous terrain in search of Colonel Fertig.

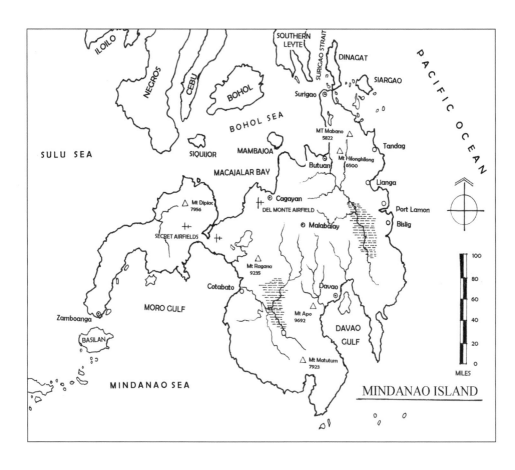

Chapter Six

RAISING "JUANITA"

Entering the jungle the men followed jungle trails down steep embankments and sharp stoned gravel gullies, using vines to pull themselves up steep inclines. The humidity was almost one hundred percent, and the slightest effort caused sweat to roll down their backs. The few gently sloped inclines gave the men a chance to talk, but most times were spent helping one another up and down the steep inclines, "huffing and puffing" along.

When they neared the Agusan river tributary they barrowed a barota and moved down stream. It was a welcome respite, and gave their sore feet an opportunity to recover. Crossing the Agusan they left the baroto at a barrio, and once again entered the jungle, following a trail. Lang remembered the difficulty of cutting a trail when heading east, and found following an existing trail better to his disposition. It was still tough going.

Once in the province of Misamis Oriental they ran into Filipinos who directed them toward the American camp. The final directions took them to a village of hastily constructed huts where they met their first American, Lieutenant Colonel McLeish, who led them to the compound. There they met Colonel Clyde Childress, six other Americans, and many armed Filipino soldiers.

The welcome was warm and friendly, as they were truly happy to see each other. Childress and McLeish encouraged the men to join them, in fact begged the men to join them. They were contending with several rebel bands in the area that were in a constant state of conflict, fighting each other and causing the unnecessary killing of troops and a few civilians. The rebel bands, headed by politicians trying to gain prestige, wanted to build dictatorial control over their provinces. It severely hampered the efforts of legitimate Filipinos and Americans wanting to combine groups to fight a common enemy, the Japanese invaders.

The principal intent of this organization was to unite these disparate groups. Colonel Fertig, the ranking American officer on the island, asked his commanders to contact every organization to join him in a combined effort. Their interest was not only harassing the enemy, but in setting up observation posts to track enemy ground, navy and air movement in order to anticipate enemy activity. They were to establish radio contact with Australia and report these movements, in preparation of the invasion to retake the islands.

Colonel Fertig had successfully evaded the Japanese to begin building his network. His Division Headquarters was in Misamis Occidental on the western peninsula, where there were several secret airfields. Although it was isolated from the main body of the island, it afforded Colonel Fertig a variety of operational advantages. Before entering service, Colonel Fertig was the president of the Colorado School of Mines. Because of his capabilities and organizational skills, he was enormously successful in uniting the soldiers on the island for a concentrated effort. He was able to do so because his staff made contact with General MacArthur in Australia, who promised delivery of supplies, guns, ammunition, clothing, medicine, and radios: everything it would take to equip a fighting force. When a submarine delivered the first supplies to the islands the disparate groups saw the wisdom of joining the main group to have access to guns and ammunition. They were soon working with troops under Colonel Fertig's leadership.

One of the basic needs for distributing these supplies would be boats to skirt the islands, and which could haul a larger capacity of gear. Since there were few roads and fewer vehicles, distributing larger quantities of supplies inland without pack animals and roads was too difficult to accomplish. Transporting supplies by water to selected sites close to interior trails would be the preferred system.

Lang, trained to work with aircraft engines, had gained valuable experience early in life by being raised on an Iowa farm. He was resourceful in solving problems and realistic in understanding the nature of the problem. Because of Lang's mechanical aptitude, Colonel Childress assigned him to look around the islands for motor launches that could be quickly repaired and put into service. In addition, he assigned Waldo Neveling to assist Lang in his effort.

Waldo Neveling was an interesting character, and would work closely with Lang for the next year. Born in Germany, Waldo had limited schooling, was self-educated and with experience became a master mechanic. He read every book, newspaper, or magazine he could get his hands on. He became a soldier of fortune at the age of thirteen. While still a teenager, he went to China to work on mechanical devices related to mining and pumping water, working there several years. The experience gained in China was the primary source of his engineering training. When the Japanese invaded China, Waldo observed how they treated the Chinese. After the "Rape of Nanking," when literally hundreds of thousands of people were violated, mutilated and killed, Waldo developed an intense hatred of the Japanese. Waldo then went to the Philippines where he consulted on gold mining operations, and when the Japanese invaded, remained to fight them. Waldo loved Germany. He spoke German, English with just a trace of an accent, some Chinese, and Tagalog, the main dialect of the Philippines. He loved the Filipinos, although his directions often included, "You bloody bastard! Do as I tell you!" (They usually did!) Waldo was in his forties, Lang in his early twenties, and they got along extremely well.

When the Japanese first landed on Mindanao, Waldo worked with them for a year or so, continuing to work in the gold mine, and had their confidence. In reality, he was feeding information to the guerrillas, as he had associated with a guerrilla band. One day the Japanese discovered his duplicity and threw him in prison. He escaped from the prison the day before he was scheduled to have his head cut off, and found his way to the McCarthy residence, where he met Dick Lang. Waldo had one major failing: he smoked constantly and was either looking for, or puffing on, a cigarette of any manufacture.

Lang and Neveling were assigned to find boats, any boats, which could be used to transport cargo between the islands. Waldo heard about a motor launch on Dinagat Island that might be repaired quickly since it was intentionally sunk by local Filipinos to keep the Japanese from commandeering it. Preparations were made to travel with a Filipino crew on the motor launch "Rosalia" to Dinagat. A stop on Leyte Island to make contact with guerrillas was also scheduled.

The trip to Leyte proved to be far more exciting then planned. Proceeding along the northwest coast of Mindanao, they stopped at barrios on the coast to meet with Filipino organizations during daylight, traveling mostly at night. About ten o'clock that night, the Rosalia was chugging along about one half mile from the Surigao coast when they almost ran head-on into a Japanese boat. Lang was first to notice it, so he grabbed the wheel and headed straight out to sea. The Japanese boat passed so close he could have thrown a grenade into it. The Japanese made no effort to intercept or recognize the Rosalia. Lang maintained the heading until he was two miles out, and turned the wheel over to the Filipino pilot, and told him to reset the course for Leyte. It soon clouded over and began raining, and they knew a storm was brewing. The rain was in their favor, since it would be difficult for the Japanese boat to track them down.

They saw no more of the Japanese boat, and assumed they had been mistaken for another Japanese boat, since there were a number of launches on patrol. The rain suddenly came in torrents. Lang glanced at the compass and saw that it was slowly turning around. Lang told the Filipino pilot about it but the pilot indicated the compass was no good. Waldo and Dick watched the compass for a while, trying to determine what was wrong. Waldo took the wheel, and the compass continued to move. Lang did not feel right about the compass and went outside the cabin. The rain had lifted, and he could see land to the left of the ship. Lang consulted with Waldo, who identified the land as a small island off the coast of Leyte. Lang decided to check the charts, and realized it could not be Leyte, but was the coast of Mindanao. The boat was traveling south instead of north.

Waldo and Lang were suddenly involved in a rather heated argument. Lang noticed they had just crossed their wake and reported it to Waldo, who told him he was crazy. Lang then got quite angry, went inside the cabin and awakened Captain Knortz, the ranking military officer, and discussed the matter with him. Knortz did not know Waldo very well, and was suspicious of him since he was a German citizen, questioning his trust. Captain Knortz asked Lang to take the wheel, and he soon had the launch on course. It seems the compass worked perfectly fine.

With daylight they discovered the delay had put them opposite a strongly fortified Japanese outpost in northern Suriago. They kept their fingers crossed as they proceeded in broad daylight, for fear of detection by air or by sea. No Japanese boats approached them. They reached the island of Leyte about eight o'clock that evening.

There was a well-organized guerrilla group on Leyte Island, and the guerrillas on the launch stopped for a few days to make contact with them. There they met other Americans: Lieutenant Hemmingway, who operated a coast watching station, Lieutenant Richardson, and Corporal Amrich. Lieutenant Richardson was later be immortalized in the book, "An American Guerrilla in the Philippines." Richardson knew first hand about the fine points of putting together a guerrilla operation, and experienced numerous skirmishes with the Japanese. He worked very closely with, and involved, the local Filipinos, a lesson that was not lost on Dick Lang.

The next day they left Leyte for Dinagat Island, about four hours away by launch. They traveled around the island until they located the cove where Waldo had heard the launch was sunk in shallow waters. The Rosalia landed on the island at a small barrio, and Lang began recruiting local Filipinos to assist in the undertaking to salvage the launch. Dick and Waldo decided that if the launch could be successfully raised they would repair it at that location.

Lang and Neveling devised a plan for building a tall tripod, mounting a block and tackle to supplement other lifting devices. With two hundred laborers at their disposal, it was quite an undertaking. Lang organized work crews and selected crew leaders, then assigned them specific tasks. The tripod lifted the hull high enough off the sea floor to slip ropes under it. Bamboo shafts five and six inches in diameter with their sealed air pockets were lashed with ropes on both sides of the hull. The individual bamboo trunks could be submerged underwater and tied with minimum difficulty. The combination of many air-filled bamboo stalks had tremendous lifting power. They managed to get the launch's rail to surface level and then floated it toward the shore. With pure physical pulling power they hauled it up on the shallow beach, propping it up so they would have access to the underside to make the necessary repairs.

The metal hull was in surprisingly good condition. It had been in water for several months and some of the caulking had broken down. Work crews scraped down all of the rust off the metal, and other crews replaced all the damaged wooden members. Filipino mechanics cleaned and oiled all of the moving parts. Finding fuel would normally be a problem, but earlier that month a Japanese freighter was torpedoed nearby and the local natives salvaged drums of oil and gas from the debris that floated in the area. They were willing to make it available to help the guerrillas. The work crew re-floated the launch and filled the tanks with gas.

The launch had a twenty-five horsepower Deutz semi-diesel engine. Once cleaned up, the mechanics could not get it to start, discovering that a piston cylinder leaked. They made the repairs as best they could, and had to improvise some method of starting it. Locating a long rope, they wrapped the flywheel with the rope and had natives pull the rope with a running start. For two full days, the men pulled the rope only stopping to switch to fresh crews. Finally, near the end of the second day of constant rope pulling, the engine coughed, sputtered, then banged away. All two hundred workers cheered, shouted and slapped each other on the back once the engine successfully ran. Their dedicated efforts were successful.

Lang recognized the tremendous effort expended by the Filipino workers and wanted to thank them. This called for a celebration. Lang purchased all of the available "tuba" (fermented sap from a coconut tree) in town, and gave it to the men and women who had worked so hard to retrieve and repair the launch. The natives, who knew about celebrations, brought out their home-made guitars, and several dalagas (young single ladies) from the barrio joined in. A fire pit was built on the beach, and soon lechon (roast suckling pig) was turning on a makeshift spit. The Filipinos ate, drank, danced, and carried on for the first time since the Japanese arrived.

Ernie and a few guerrillas decided to have some fun with Dick Lang, and approached him with the comment that one of the smallest dalagas wanted to dance with him. Lang explained that he was a married man and probably should not dance with the young woman. However, the tuba and the guerrillas prevailed, and Dick finally danced with the young woman. All the guerrillas had a big laugh, since the dalaga's nose barely reached Dick's belt line. Dick also had a good laugh, and made a point to dance with all the dalagas to show support for all of the natives who had helped on the recovery of the launch.

The celebration became a farewell party, because Lang and Neveling were planning to leave the next day. The workers, amidst the revelry, decided to christen the launch late in the festivities. With a full canteen of tuba, they enthusiastically christened the vessel.

They renamed the launch the "Juanita."

Dick dancing with a dalaga to show support for all of the natives who had helped on the recovery of the launch.

Chapter Seven

ON THE RECRUITING TRAIL

The next morning Dick and Waldo met with the workers of Dinagat Island to thank them and say goodbye. Lang enjoyed working with the Filipinos: they were industrious, hardworking and eager to do their best. They were a cheerful people, gregarious and anxious to please.

The origin of settlers in the Philippine Islands is sketchy, but believed to by inhabitants of Mongoloid descent that produced the Malay-related people prominent in Southeast Asia today. There are recorded instances of trading with China during the tenth century. During the fifteenth century, there was a gradual spread of Islam from Borneo. Islam was contained in the central and northern regions by the arrival of the Spanish Christians. After the landing on the islands on March 25, 1521, Ferdinand Magellan named them after Spain's King Phillip II. Three weeks after his arrival in the islands, natives killed Magellan in a battle on Mactan Island. For centuries, the Philippine Islands were the main outpost for Spain's proselytizing in Asia. Soldiers, lead by Miguel Lopez de Lagazpi, and missionaries, introduced Christianity and attempted to unify the many peoples under a central government. The Spanish Inquisition was at a high point in Europe and thousands of people were labeled as heretics and killed for the simplest of reasons. Questioning religious interpretation, taking a bath more frequently than every two weeks, or not keeping the Sabbath, were sins punishable by death. As in Central America, the conquistadors brought bitter fighting and bloodshed to the islands. The Spanish succeeded in driving the Islamic worshippers from the northern islands south to Mindanao, and soon established a Jesuit base at Zamboanga. The Spanish wanted absolute authority over the entire country, and wanted the Philippines to become the main Catholic outpost for subjugating the South Pacific. However, Islam continued in the highlands of Mindanao. The English, Dutch and Portuguese, unlike the Spanish, wanted to develop countries for economic reasons rather than religious reasons.

The Philippine Islands received supplies from ships sailing from New Spain (Mexico) that traveled nine thousand miles exposed to storms and pirates. Arrival of the ships provided subsidies and orders from the New Spain government. Any loss of ships meant a year of destitution. Foreign competition in the late 1700s helped to end the Spanish monopoly, providing a more stable economic environment. For more then two hundred years Spain maintained strict control of commerce that exchanged products between Europe/Mexico and the Philippines. Because of the high profits from China and New Spain trade, colonial officials neglected commercial development on the islands choosing to rely on subsidies from the outside world.

Manila became the colonial capitol, and imperial rule controlled the coasts, but not the southern islands and highlands where Islam was entrenched. The Viceroyalty of New Spain (now Mexico) governed the islands as well as Mexico, and introduced still another culture into the islands. Trade with China entrepreneurs, silver for silk, brought many Chinese immigrants to the islands. Intermarriage between the Spaniards and Islanders, and Chinese and Islanders, produced mestizos and developed a distinctive new culture.

Mexico's independence from Spain encouraged self-development by the mestizos who created a wealthy class, went to Europe for their education, and returned with a liberal education that fostered a sense of national identity. The Catholic Church continued to work actively in the islands with missionary priests from many countries working with the natives. They encouraged a minimum of education, and attempted to raise the religious dedication in their daily lives. The education of the priesthood from Filipino culture created an interest in the development of a more responsive religious and political outlook that encouraged native values, free of European influence. The Filipino priesthood challenged the inequality of church rankings, and the resulting discontent grew into a spirit of nationalism. This discontent inspired and was fostered by Jose Rizal, who was an advocate of peaceful reform under the colonial rulers. Unfortunately, because of his insurgence, Spanish colonial rulers executed Rizal, which started an armed revolt under Andres Bonificio. This was about the same time that America got into the act.

For thirty years, the United States had been sparring with Spain over the disposition of Cuba, off the coast of Florida. During the early 1890's, there was an insurrection by Cubans fighting the repressive control by the Spanish Army. As the army increased the number of "arrests, seizures, searches, tortures, and executions," the American press took up Cuba's cause, inciting and infuriating American citizens, and encouraging a fighting response to the Spanish repression. In one of the more interesting aspects of American history, the press wanted a war and created the circumstances for it. The new American warship, the USS Maine, was ordered to Havana, Cuba, where it unfortunately struck a mine in the harbor and sank. To the cry of "Remember the Maine: To hell with Spain," America prepared for war.

After a short period, on April 11, 1898, president William McKinley asked Congress for war powers to fight against Spain, and Congress agreed. A ground war started in Cuba, but interestingly enough, the main naval action took place in the Philippine Islands. Before dawn on May 1, 1898, the small American Asiatic squadron of six ships, commanded by Commodore George Dewey, steamed past the silent Spanish guns on the island of Corregidor into Manila Bay to face a larger Spanish force at anchor. At 5:40 am, Commodore Dewey gave his historic command to the flagship commander, Charles Vernon Gridley, "You may fire when ready, Gridley!"

By 7:45 am, they completely silenced the Spanish ships, with three warships on fire. The Americans withdrew, ate breakfast, and once more entered the harbor to silence the big shore batteries on Corregidor. That evening the American fleet anchored in Manila Harbor and the navy bands "played their usual evening concert."

After the U.S. victory in Manila Bay, Nationalist Emilio Aguinaldo declared independence from Spain and declared himself the president of a provisional republic. At first he supported the American involvement in helping to develop the Philippine Islands. However, when the Americans instituted certain practices he became incensed that the U.S. would be occupying the Philippines as the Spanish had, and started a full-scale guerrilla action against the Americans. The Americans instead of being liberators turned to conquest. They defeated the insurgents in a series of battles fought on various islands and locations: Manila, Malolos, Iloilo, Vigan, Tacloban and Barceloneta. Aguinaldo, unhappy that America was seizing the country, staged several bloody raids at Leculan, Tinuba and Santa Cruz, but was captured on Luzon at Palanan. After one or two more skirmishes, the fighting concluded July 4, 1902.

The U.S. bought and redistributed church-owned lands. Unfortunately, most of it went to the large landowners. Sanitation and health care were of interest, and U.S. aid was available to improve all facilities. A few roads, a stable currency, and inter-island shipping encouraged free trade. English introduced in the schools replaced Spanish, and brought greater linguistic unity to all of the islands. Access to items manufactured in America lead the Filipinos to ignore industrial development, and concentrate on an agrarian society. Mining and export crops became the main focus of their economy, and an essentially U.S. based economy was developed. The citizens were still interested in independence, and in 1935, the Filipinos accepted a U.S. offer of sovereignty following a ten-year commonwealth status. The insurgent Aguinaldo would live to see Philippine independence after World War II.

Lack of inter-island communication and a uniform road system preserved the agrarian nature of most of the citizens. It was this rural characteristic reflecting the trusting nature of the Filipino people, that Lang found so engaging.

The men said their goodbyes to the citizens who had been so helpful in raising the Juanita, left the southern Dinagat Island, and proceeded north along the shoreline. They stopped at a good-sized community on the north shore, only to discover it burned to the ground. An armed crew cautiously went ashore to inspect the damage, but there were no natives to be found. Two local inhabitants hiding in the bush finally made an appearance, and approached the landing party when they discovered the visitors were "white men." When the two realized the visitors were Americans, local people poured out of the woods in the most inquisitive manner, and welcomed them as close friends. When Lang inquired what had happened to their town, the natives excitedly told their story.

A few days earlier a Japanese transport was traveling in the area and anchored about a mile from shore. The townspeople fled to the hills, fearing an invasion. Four local Filipino army soldiers who had not surrendered returned to their hometown with their rifles and ten rounds of ammunition each. Instead of taking to the hills when the transport anchored, the men lay in the weeds along the beach to observe the Japanese intentions. The Japanese lowered two small launches with about twenty men in each boat, and headed for the shore. As they approached land, one launch was following a short distance behind the other. The Japanese did not know the channel that lead to the beach, and when they were about forty yards out both launches ran aground in shallow water.

The four young Filipino soldiers saw the Japanese had not only run aground, but were perfect targets. It was a rare opportunity. As the Japanese jumped out of their boat to try to dislodge it, the four soldiers loaded their rifles and proceeded to pick them off, one by one, until they had killed all of the enemy in the launches.

When the Japanese on the large boat saw what was happening, they uncovered their five-inch cannon and proceeded to shell the town, setting it on fire. They did not leave until they had leveled or burned every building.

Lang's main reason for stopping at that town was to locate more fuel and oil. The locals had only one barrel of oil and passed it on to the launch. The natives informed Lang that more oil and fuel was available on Siaragao Island, which was about a day's travel by launch. The men spent the night as guests of the community in their temporary housing in the jungle. The shelling of the town had frightened members of the community, but they were already planning the reconstruction of their village. Men were scouting the jungle for building materials that would let them start rebuilding.

Early the next morning Lang and his crew loaded their gear and left the beach, carefully avoiding the shallows. The sea was relatively calm and they made good time heading toward Siaragao. Following the natives' directions, they entered the mouth of a large river, proceeding nicely, when their launch got hung-up on a large underwater rock. The men rocked the launch and tried to pole it off without any luck. Finally, the entire crew jumped into the river and managed to push the launch backwards off the rock. The men climbed back into the launch, and as they were putting on their clothes, Lang noticed three of the largest sharks he had ever seen swimming around the boat. Lang pointed them out to Waldo, and they both decided they would never go swimming there again.

It was now low tide, and after traveling a mile upstream, the river was too shallow to continue. The men decided to anchor the Juanita and proceed up river in a lighter boat. They got into a small baroto and paddled up the river to the town of Numaneia, where more fuel was supposed to be available. They located a barrel of diesel fuel, and arranged with the natives to have it loaded in the baroto. It was late afternoon, and they decided to return to the launch, which was about a mile downstream but a mile from the river's entrance. As they proceeded down the river they sighted a Japanese boat about seven or eight miles away headed directly toward their brand new Juanita.

The only option was to paddle as fast as they could to reach the launch, load the fuel, and get away as fast as possible. They had left a Filipino mechanic on board, and when he saw the approaching Japanese boat, he tried to start the engine using compressed air to turn the engine. However, he was using up valuable air pressure and not having any success starting the engine. The baroto reached the launch in record time, and Waldo immediately jumped on to start the engine. Dick and two Filipinos were to load the fuel barrel aboard. They slipped two ropes around the barrel and tried pulling it into the launch. The three small Filipinos struggled to get the barrel out of the baroto, but did not have the strength to get it over the edge of the launch. Waldo managed to get the motor going, as the Japanese boat kept getting closer.

Lang, in desperation and with an adrenaline rush, jumped into the baroto, lifted the barrel and threw it into the launch. As he pushed the barrel, the baroto went in the opposite direction, and Lang belly-flopped into the water. Remembering the sharks they had seen earlier, Lang pulled himself out of the water in a flurry of scrambling. He was taking no chances. Sometime later he tried to lift the barrel, and found he could not get it off the deck.

The tide now permitted the launch to move up river, and since it drew a shallower profile then the Japanese boat, moved upstream to find shelter in a small cove. The Japanese boat passed by without firing a shot.

The next few days were spent traveling around Siaragao Island contacting small guerrilla units. Lang gave them instructions to send representatives to the division headquarters for further directions in order to organize a combined effort against the Japanese. The individual bands of local men showed great interest in working with Colonel Fertig in his military effort.

From Siaragao Island, they proceeded to Claver, a barrio on the northeast coast of Mindanao. Captain Knortz set up headquarters and formed a new regiment at that location. Since the launch was needed to transfer cargo from submarines, Captain Knorz sent the launch Rosalio back to division headquarters. As a result, Lang spent the next few weeks with Captain Knortz along the east coast of Mindanao contacting and organizing all guerrilla units into the new 114th Regiment forming on the Mindanao east coast, part of the 110th Division of the 10th Military District. Colonel Fertig was to be the commander of the 10th Military District as authorized by General MacArthur.

Most of the guerrilla units contacted were willing to join under American leadership, particularly since new supplies would be arriving from Australia. However, there were still several groups of a fiercely independent nature looting towns on the island. Since they were not interested in cooperation, Colonel Fertig decided to confront them with force. There were several skirmishes in the jungles, and the Colonel's troops managed to overcome the disorganized groups and relieve them of their weapons. Colonel Fertig gave them an option: join the 114th Regiment or banishment into the jungle with no weapons.

Colonel Fertig had his headquarters on the northwest side of Mindanao in the Misamis Occidental province, east of Cagayan, but he traveled extensively about the island. The Colonel contacted General MacArthur, informing him of the success in organizing the disparate groups of insurgents. MacArthur responded by sending supplies from the Southwest Pacific (SOWESPAC) headquarters via submarine, and many future deliveries would soon be on their way.

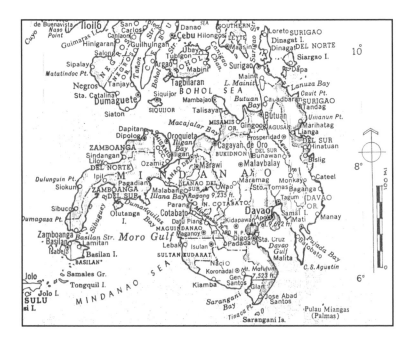

Chapter Eight

HAVERHILL

Haverhill, Marshall County IA, is a long way from Mindanao in the Philippine Islands. It would have been impossible to predict that Dick Lang would spend three and a half years of his young life so far from home. Still, most of the young people who grew up in Haverhill moved from home to seek their fortune, find employment, or just get away. It is not that Haverhill in the 1930's was not a good place to grow up. People looked after one another, families cooperated, and everyone knew everyone else. If a child got into the least bit of trouble, the whole town helped to straighten that youngster out. Still, growing up in Haverhill did not have much to keep the young folks there. Leaving home for a larger city during the great depression offered far more opportunities.

Haverhill was one of the small communities established in Iowa in the 1880's by railroad traffic. Early trains were powered by steam engines that were not the most efficient. Trains had enough water capacity to feed the steam boilers for seven to ten miles before the water supply needed refilling. As a result, Iowa community patterns developed every seven or eight miles. It was also a comfortable distance for farmers to haul their farm products by horse drawn wagons to the railroad station for shipping to the larger markets.

East coast land investors would buy a tract of land from the railroad builders and subdivide it, selling it to entrepreneurs who would market it to retailers who catered to the developing farm trade. Fortunes were made and lost in small town land development schemes throughout the Midwest.

As boiler technology improved, the distance between water stops became fourteen miles, then forty miles, and finally the diesel engine created interstate fueling stations. Small town survival refocused on serving the farm trade, local educational institutions, or as a center for religious training.

Haverhill in early 1900 was a bustling town of three hundred fifty people. It had a lumberyard, elevator, grocery stores, a blacksmith, and livery stables. Only a few miles south of the county seat town of Marshalltown, the community was served by the Milwaukee Railroad main line, with several freight and passenger trains stopping every day. Haverhill was also the site of a large Catholic church that reflected the large Catholic population in the area.

During the 1860's Iowa saw the influx of many German immigrants who were fleeing the constant small wars and civil unrest that plagued Europe at that time. They located in Indiana and Illinois, moving further west as land became available. A large German Catholic settlement at Dyersville attracted many settlers, and when that community became crowded settlers started new enclaves in the rich, black soil of central Iowa. Most of the Haverhill settlers relocated from Dyersville IA, Luxembourg IA, and Galena IL. When it was time to build a new worship edifice, the settlers copied the huge church in Dyersville, building only one tower instead of two. It was a most impressive structure, and was the focal point of the energy and vitality of the farming community.

Sylvester Lang and his wife, Anna Oetker Lang, operated a large farm two miles from Haverhill. Consistent with work on the farm, it was necessary to have a large family in order to meet the intense farm labor requirements. A large family was also consistent with practices in the Catholic faith at that time, to be fruitful and multiply. Sylvester and Anna entered into both practices with religious fervor and spirit, and raised a family of fifteen children. Times were tough as America entered the depression, but Sylvester was a strict disciplinarian, and every child did his or her part to contribute to the family's well-being. The farm produced meat, vegetables, chickens, eggs, milk, butter, and other necessities for a healthy life. The education, entertainment, social life and work ethic centered on the church and churchly attitudes.

Dick Lang was the fifth child of Sylvester and Anna, and had his first blurred look of Iowa on December 18, 1918. The first few years of his education were in a one-room school, but in keeping with the local custom, he attended the parochial school in Haverhill. The nearest parochial high school was St. Mary's in Marshalltown, where he commuted with other local students. There was no time for sports or activities, since he had to hurry home to help with the chores. His main form of recreation, as well as a source of spending money, was trapping. It was something he could do in the early morning before chores, before leaving for school. There were plenty of animals in the rural area: skunks, muskrat, mink and an occasional fox. During the summer, he trapped pocket gophers because there was a ten-cent bounty on each pair of front feet delivered to the county courthouse. It exposed Dick to the out-of-doors in all kinds of weather. He learned to skin the animals and store them properly to get the best price. It gave him the responsibility of preparing the traps, study- ing the habitat of the animals, and checking them regularly. Little did he realize how much this would prepare him for coping with unusual situations later in his military experience.

Dick graduated from St. Mary's in the spring of 1936. He had grown to a strapping six foot three inches, considered very tall at that time. He was well coordinated, even though he could not participate in sports activities because of his responsibilities on the farm. In addition, Sylvester Lang considered sports a waste of time.

Dick Lang's first full time job after graduation was in the Marshalltown Hospital, working as a stoker, shoveling coal into the big boilers that provided heat and energy for the building. It was a dirty job with the coal dust swirling about, and extremely physical. The time intervals between the banking of fires in the boilers were spent observing the many activities that define a hospital, which he thoroughly enjoyed.

Recruiters encouraged him to enlist in the National Guard. Again, it was an opportunity to grow, to learn, and use his time to good advantage: he joined Company H, 168th Infantry, stationed at the armory in Marshalltown where he served for three years. Dick entered the guard and learned military discipline and the succession of military command. It also expanded his education in organization and "how things work."

After two years stoking the fires at St. Mary's Hospital in Marshalltown, he started working for a local roofing contractor. It was another dirty job, working with hot tar, carrying rolls of felt, and mopping hot asphalt and tar on roofs. It was a toasty warm job on cool spring and fall mornings, but beastly hot during the summertime, standing on a heat absorbing black surface spreading more hot black material. However, during the roofing season he worked long hours, and the additional income was welcome.

On one occasion, Dick was visiting old friends at St. Mary's hospital, and ran into a friend, Lillian Carmody who worked as a nurse at Mercy Hospital, but who was visiting her mother. Lillian began teasing him about being a "big good-looking farm boy with no social life." She suggested a double date with her sister, who worked as a receptionist-secretary for Gibbs-Cook Heavy Equipment Company in Des Moines. Dick was reluctant at first, but finally gave in, and Lillian made the arrangements.

Margaret Carmody was raised on a farm near Zearing IA. She attended a one-room school through the eighth grade, a common practice in those days. The ninth and tenth grades were spent in Lincoln Township High School, in Story County. However, Margaret wanted to learn shorthand and typing, so she arranged to live with an aunt and uncle in Nevada. She would attend the Nevada High School Monday morning through Friday, returning home on the weekends. After graduating from high school, she attended Capitol City Commercial College in Des Moines, where she learned the bookkeeping skills needed to work in an established business. Bookkeeping, teaching and library work were some of the few highly respected, but low paying, jobs available to women at that time. America was starting to recover from the depression, and women had not entered the workforce in great numbers in defense work as they would after the war started. Margaret was pretty, pert, and vivacious. For Margaret the prospect of a date with the tall, handsome farm boy was titillating.

Margaret and Dick joined Lillian and her husband-to-be Cecil Botts for a movie, after which they went to a local hangout, "Rosie's Tenderloin." Rosie's just happened to have the best malts and tenderloins in the whole "United States of Marshall County." Rosie was very familiar with the Lang boys. When they entered the shop, she hid the catsup since the boys devoured enormous quantities of catsup on everything edible. It was an evening of giggling, and flirting, and teasing. When they parted, Dick said, "I'll call you sometime."

A month or so passed, and petite Margaret had not heard from Dick, so she decided to get his attention. On St. Valentines Day Dick received a large white envelope that contained a big red heart. Written inside the card was a rather direct message. "You said you were going to call me! You are nothing but a dirty double-crosser!!!"

Dick, rather awkwardly, made a phone call, and they started seeing one another more regularly. Rosie's Tenderloin continued to be the favorite hangout, and Rosie continued to hide the catsup.

The summer of 1940 was idyllic enough in Central Iowa, but across the ocean in Europe, serious conflicts were developing. Germany was pressing hard to expand into southern Europe, and England was one of the few countries trying to resolve the political dilemma. Dick realized that if he were going to be drafted into service, he would rather choose his type of service. He had a friend who had moved to Riverside CA, and after consulting with him, decided to drive to California to consider the options. Since his days shoveling coal at St. Mary's, he had been interested in things medical.

Dick and two friends from the Marshalltown area put their belongings in the back of a Model A Ford and started for the west coast.

Dick and Margaret discussed the possibility of what might be in store for the future, but made no specific plans. They were semi-serious about their future together, but were still hesitant about commitment. There was no hesitancy on Margaret's part.

Dick enlisted in the Army, first served in a medical installation, and then transferred to Headquarters Company of the 19th Bombardment Group to play basketball. He completed training at the Curtis-Wright Technical Institute for Aircraft Maintenance receiving Very Satisfactory in all of his classes. Now it was time to perform.

The 19th Bombardment Group was then sent to Albuquerque NM for assembly. It seems the unit was selected for a six-month maneuvers in the Philippine Islands to service the B-17s that would soon be arriving. Margaret was still working as a secretary for Gibbs-Cook in Des Moines, and Dick called to explain that he would soon be going overseas. Margaret declared without a moment's hesitation that she wanted to get married before he left.

The 19th BG Chaplain, Father Joseph LeFleur, had become a good friend of Lang and discouraged Dick from any marriage before going overseas. Dick called Margaret and tried to convince her it might not be the best in the long term. Margaret was firm about her intentions and refused to be dissuaded. She was determined they would wed: she had purchased a wedding dress. Seeking reinforcement, Margaret called Dick's parents and pleaded her case. Anna and Sylvester gave her their whole-hearted support.

Margaret Carmody wasted no time. She would catch a train to Albuquerque, where they could be married before he went overseas. He would only be gone six months. There was no prospect for war. He would be safe in the Philippine Islands. There was no reason to wait.

It was Margaret's first train ride. She packed her suitcase and boarded the Rock Island Rocket for Kansas City. She changed trains in the huge Union train station filled with soldiers and sailors in transit, and families saying their goodbyes. It was an immense, grand space that made her feel tiny and alone. In Kansas City she boarded a Missouri Pacific train for the ride south, and

Margaret and Dick Lang's wedding picture, September 17, 1941. The wedding dress arrived just in time.

St.Charles Catholic Church in Albuquerque NM, where Dick and Margaret were married. Father Lefleur was very busy that day performing eight wedding ceremonies.

would transfer on one other rail line before arriving in Albuquerque. It took two days sitting upright in the chair car, eating only one meal per day in the elegant dining car. It was a big world outside of Des Moines.

Dick met her at the train station in Albuquerque in a happy and tearful reunion. He had located one half of a furnished duplex they could rent for two weeks. A Private First Class did not make very much money, but Dick managed to work out a deal with a fellow soldier who was renting both units.

When unpacking her clothes Margaret made a shocking discovery. The day Margaret boarded the train her roommates had thrown a surprise shower for her, and she had shown them her wedding dress. After the shower, her mother came by to see the dress. After showing it off, Margaret slipped it under the bed while she was packing, and promptly forgot about it. When she was unpacking her suitcase in the duplex, she discovered that in her haste she had forgotten to pack the wedding dress. She immediately called her roommate, since four girls were living together in an apartment, who retrieved the dress, packed it, and stood by the mailbox until the mailman arrived, to make certain it would be in the first mail. With perfect timing, the dress arrived in Albuquerque the day before the wedding.

Margaret and Dick were married in St. Charles Catholic Church, Albuquerque, on September 17, 1941, by Dick's friend, the 19th BG Chaplin, Lieutenant Father Joseph LeFleur. Their witnesses were Sergeant Bill Jones, a soldier friend of Dicks, and Jerri Monaghan, the wife of another soldier friend. Father LeFleur's advice about marriage before going overseas was generally ignored as he married seven other couples that same day.

Dick and Margaret were able to spend ten evenings together after Dick completed his daily military responsibilities. They did not consider the possibility of Margaret becoming a war widow since Lang was, more or less, a non-combatant. She would be a soldier's wife: honor, cherish, obey, and dutifully write every day.

The day before the 19th BG was scheduled to ship out to San Francisco, Margaret and Dick went to the train station, said their tearful goodbyes, and lifted her suitcase aboard the train. It was a long two-day trip back to Marshalltown. It was sad and happy, crowded and alone, full of love and trepidation. The good news was their separation would only be for six months.

Margaret Carmody Lang would not see or hear from her husband again for three and one-half years.

The intensity of preparing for overseas duty did not permit filing the paperwork for recording the marriage of Margaret and

Dick with the military, and as a result, Dick's parents remained on the record as next of kin. Seven months later when Dick decided not to surrender to the Japanese and fade into the jungle, it was Anna Oetker Lang who received the telegram:

THE ARMY OF THE UNITED STATES REGRETS TO INFORM YOU THAT YOUR SON PRIVATE FIRST CLASS RICHARD LANG IS MISSING IN ACTION IN THE PHILIPPINE ISLANDS. YOU WILL BE INFORMED IF ANY ADDITIONAL WORD IS RECEIVED.

When the telegram arrived, Margaret was at work in Des Moines. When Anna called she immediately returned to the Lang residence to be with the family. There was always the prospect Dick was safe. This unsure distant hope prevailed until, over two years later Margaret received a letter from a returned guerrilla officer who wrote, "I have seen Dick Lang. He is alive and well. I cannot say where he is."

Echoes of Carmel

Published by the Students of Mt. Carmel Schools in Louisiana

New Orleans: Lakeview, St. Dominic, St. James Major and St. Augustine Schools; Lafayette,
Thibodaux, New Iberia, Abbeville, Rayne, Paincourtville, Westwego, and Carencro

| VOLUME XVII | NEW ORLEANS, LA., APRIL, 1943 | No. 7 |

NEWS OF FATHER LAFLEUR BRINGS JOY TO LOUISIANIANS

FATHER LAFLEUR

(Continued from Page 1)

hind. On hearing this, the young priest made his decision to stay with his men, because he felt that there was more need for his services on that lonely isle than in the States.

Still Courageous

The informant also added that Father Lafleur has been doing wonderful work among the army boys. He related an incident that occurred when the group was being transported to another island. The ship was torpedoed and it was Father Lafleur who, in his usual calm and courageous way, saw to it that every man left the ship.

The comment made often by those who know Father Lafleur when they heard the story of his heroism was, "That's just like him," because they remember well his generosity and spirit of self-sacrifice. While he was assistant pastor in Abbeville, Father Lafleur was all to all. For this and many other reasons he has received a permanent place in the hearts of the people. Everyone is sure that, as his commanding officer once said, "he is everything that we desire in an army chaplain."

Therese Harrington, '44.

FATHER LAFLEUR

Reported Missing A Year Ago

Students of Abbeville Carmel, together with the people of Abbeville and south Louisiana, are rejoicing over the news that Rev. Joseph V. Lafleur, chaplain and first lieutenant in the United States army, who was reported missing in the Philippine Islands, is safe at a secret base in the Pacific.

The good news was the result of an effort made by Miss Mildred Lafleur to procure authentic information of the whereabouts of her brother. Upon hearing that the bombardment group of which Father Lafleur was the chaplain had arrived in the States, Miss Lafleur wrote to the group commanding officer asking for news of Father Lafleur. The commanding officer turned the letter over to one of the chaplain's best friends in the group, and he in turn sent the information that everyone was so eager to hear.

Stayed At Post

At the time the bombardment group left the island base their chaplain, who received the Distinguished Service Cross for bravery under fire, could have left, too, along with the other officers. When the time of departure arrived, Father Lafleur asked about the men who were not leaving the base. He was told that it was not possible to evacuate all the men and many of them would have to stay be-

(Continued on Page 7)

Chapter Nine

FATHER LEFLEUR

First Lieutenant Joseph LeFleur, Chaplain of the 19th Bomber Group, was very close to his soldiers. Dick Lang was a regular attendee when he served Mass, and they became close friends. Although Father LeFleur attempted to discourage Margaret from getting married prior to Dick's overseas duty, he happily performed the ceremony.

Father LaFleur traveled on the Maayon from Baatan to Cagayan, Mindanao with members of the 19th Bomber Group. Joseph LaFleur, raised in the parochial schools of New Orleans, was the former assistant pastor at Abbyville LA. He celebrated daily Mass at the airbase and was respected and appreciated by all the men, regardless of their respective faiths. His southern demeanor endeared him to the men in the bomber group, and he was conspicuously visible at jevery gathering.

FATHER LAFLEUR

When the troops were ordered to surrender to the Japanese, Dick Lang begged Father LeFleur to accompany him into the interior, but the chaplain felt he should be with the majority of the men until they were released by the American forces.

When the soldiers surrendered, the Japanese marched them to temporary barracks used by the Filipino army. A stockade was built nearby, and the base enclosed with a barbed wire fence. As the men marched to the barracks, the Japanese soldiers attempted to relieve the American and Filipino captives of their watches, rings, and other valuables. When some men refused they were pulled out of line, hit with a gun butt, and kicked in the stomach until they willingly gave up their possessions. It was the prisoners' first exposure to the brutality many prisoners would experience during their incarceration.

The first few months several prisoners managed to escape from the compound. The Japanese solved the escape problem by organizing the camp in groups of ten prisoners, with all ten to be accounted for in a daily roll call. If one prisoner escaped, the remaining nine in that group would be executed. It stopped most attempts to escape.

The prisoners were made up of mechanics, ordinance men, engineers, medics, band members, pilots, artillery, navy men; the entire spectrum of service personnel. Some were better equipped to deal with the circumstances of incarceration than others. For food, the prisoners received one handful of rice each day. The water from the local well was brackish, so the men caught and saved rainwater for drinking. After a few months prisoners began to die from poor diet, lack of medication, or physical abuse.

The Japanese staff organized the barracks by rank and age. It appeared to help the prisoners to associate with an identifiable similar group. Separated from the Americans, the Filipinos were physically treated much worse than the Americans were. As poorly as the Americans were treated, it must have been frightful for those imprisoned on their native soil.

The prisoners performed menial labor in the area, usually taken out in groups. It was difficult for the prisoners to understand what the Japanese wanted them to do, since few of the captors spoke English. A Japanese soldier would take the men to a ditch, explain what he needed in Japanese, and wave his hands. The Americans were severely beaten if they did not understand what the soldier intended them to do. Sooner or later work would start and tasks were accomplished. The bruises and lacerations remained.

The Japanese needed men to work in the rice fields in southern Mindanao, so a large number of prisoners were herded aboard a freighter in Cagayan and transported to Davao, on the southern shore. The prisoners marched to the Davao Penal Colony where they lived with the prisoners in their cells. Conditions were crowded and the food was terrible. However, for a change, drinking water was readily available.

Mt. Apo, the highest volcanic mountain in the Philippine Islands, reaching 9,620 feet, is located just outside Davao. Rice paddies climb the foothills of the mountain and spread out on the surrounding plains. Most of the prisoners were forced to work in the rice paddies, preparing the soil, planting the rice and harvesting the rice. Planting rice at different time intervals meant the harvesting of rice went on continuously, and food would be available for the prisoners.

Some of the men worked cutting abaca, a hemp plant used for making rope. The long fibers of the plant stalks were individually separated and hung on simple wooden racks to dry. The fibers were then bundled for shipment to a manufacturing plant where the fibers were twisted and woven into long strands of rope. The huge coils of rope were trucked to the docks, where they were distributed throughout the Philippine Islands. All of the operations used forced prisoner labor.

The prisoners continued to receive one handful of rice daily. They learned that watercress and some grasses that grew along the irrigation ditches were edible, and sneaked a mouthful whenever they could. On one trip to the abaca field, the prisoners passed a group of coconut palms where a large number of nuts had fallen to the ground. The prisoners begged to have the coconuts that were wasting away, to drink the milk and eat the coconut meat. The Japanese beat them off and made them continue on their way.

As the men's clothing deteriorated they resorted to wearing a G-string with a measure of cloth pulled through the front and back. The basic cloth was comfortable to work in during the heat of the day, was easily washed in the irrigation ditches, but little comfort during the chill of the evening.

Many of the prisoners craved cigarettes, particularly since they were not available. A favorite trick of the guards was to light a cigarette, take several puffs, then discard it. When a prisoner would jump to grab the cigarette butt, the guard would stomp on the prisoner's hand and laugh uproariously. The physical abuse by the guards depended upon the mood of the guard inflicting the punishment. It could vary from a simple cuffing to a beating resulting in death.

Father LeFleur did his best to keep the spirits of the men positive. The longer they were prisoners, the more they talked about Americans winning the war and of being rescued by the return of General MacArthur. The men sought hope in the smallest sign, and relied on each other to keep spirits buoyed.

The Japanese had an airstrip near Lasang and selected six hundred men to travel there to make repairs from recent damage by the Americans bombers. Since the prisoners were doing hard labor using shovels, the men thought their diet might improve, but it remained the same. Repairing the airstrip meant the Japanese were concerned about the increasing air activity by American planes, and it spurred the prisoner's hopes for the return of American soldiers.

The Japanese decided to evacuate all of the prisoners from southern Mindanao. Word leaked out that there was going to be a prisoner exchange, and once again, the prisoners grasped for the hope of the prospect of surviving the war. In reality, the Japanese needed physical laborers on the farms in Japan and in the coalmines in Manchuria.

A decrepit, rusty freighter arrived at the docks of Davao, and the prisoners were marched to the dock, tethered on a continuous rope. An attempt at escape would have been futile since the men were weak and malnourished; still, the Japanese took no chances. They were marched aboard the freighter, and forced to climb down a steel ladder, several cargo decks down. The men were packed in the lowest hold so tight they could not move. They finally arranged to sit down, with their legs apart so other soldiers could sit between their legs. When the hold was full, the sick and wounded were lowered in a cargo net and squeezed into place. The temperature was over one hundred degrees, and the men gasped for air. Finally, heavy planks covered the hatch, spaced three or four inches apart for air movement, and lashed into place with ropes. When the loading was nearing completion an American plane flew over, and a tarpaulin was thrown over the opening, closing off all outside air movement. The men below gagged from the stale air, unable to catch their breath. When the plane left the area, the canvas was removed permitting some air circulation.

The freighter left Davao for sea and zigzagged a course for five days. The trip normally would take twenty-four hours, but since the Japanese ships were being torpedoed with great regularity, the freighter traveled only at night, staying in bays during the day. Records show over three hundred freight boats sunk in that area during the war.

The Japanese lowered two buckets for the men to use as a toilet, and when they were full, took delight in swinging them about and spilling the contents as they were pulled upward. Rice and water were also lowered in buckets, and the men struggled to get their share. Father LeFleur separated the men into groups of twenty, as it would be easier to distribute the food and water evenly. Each man got a spoonful of rice and a spoonful of water. The prisoners respected Father LeFleur, for his fairness and because of this, the Japanese gave him more leeway than they did the other prisoners.

After five days travel, the freighter landed at Zamboanga, on the western peninsula of Mindanao. There the prisoners transferred to the Shinyo Maru, another ancient seagoing freighter. As the men walked the gangway from the first boat, they were hosed down with seawater, a semi-shower that felt wonderful to the men who had been locked in close quarters in the ship's hold. Once again, they descended a ladder below decks, to the same over-crowded conditions. As they left Zamboanga harbor their biggest fear now was suffocation. They realized there would be no prisoner exchange.

The freighter had been traveling about five days in the open water in a small convoy when around mid-day the prisoners heard a machine gun chatter. Then an explosion shook the slow moving freighter, and water began rushing into the ship. The planks were blown off the hatch opening, letting in a stream of sunlight, and ropes from the planks dangled into darkness below. Those with the strength climbed the ropes to the deck, to find it awash in blood. As the ship listed some prisoners managed to crawl up the bulkhead and out through the cargo door. Prisoners remaining below, were calmed by Father LeFleur who quietly, peacefully, began, " Our Father, who art in Heaven..." as the water continued to rise. Of the six hundred seventy-five prisoners aboard the Shiniyo Maru, only eighty-three survived. They managed to swim to a nearby island, rescued by Filipino guerrillas who nursed them back to health and ultimately returned them to U.S. authorities.

On September 7, 1944, the Japanese freighter Shiniyo Maru was sunk by a torpedo fired from an American submarine.

Chapter Ten

PORT LAMON

Early in July 1943, Dick Lang received a message to meet with Colonel Childress at his headquarters. Lang was working the territory, visiting groups convincing them to join the fight against the Japanese, under the Mindanao command of Colonel Fertig. Occasionally a few supplies arrived for Colonel Childress from submarine deliveries, but nothing substantial or in quantity. Communications were much better now and more help would be on the way. Colonel Childress met with Lang and informed him that Division Commander Colonel Fertig wanted to meet with him, and where the Colonel could be located.

Lang traveled two weeks through the jungle to meet with Colonel Fertig, who was very welcoming. They sat in his headquarters building at a table, and an assistant brought them a cup of what tasted like coffee. The building blended into the local housing; bamboo construction and palm roof with swalley walls, so it would not be spotted by a reconnaissance plane flying over.

Fertig was very friendly, but suddenly put on his military face. "Lang, we have made tremendous progress here in eastern Mindanao. Your efforts have been very promising and much appreciated. Recent communications from General MacArthur, however, tell us they do not care how many Japanese we kill. They are much more interested in what we see. They want reports on troop movements, but want more emphasis on shipping and air flights. They want to know what the Japs are up to, where they are going, and in what numbers."

Lang moved uneasily. "Are there radios available?"

"We are putting together several teams for scouting and observing. That is not what I need you for. You have many talents. You can organize, you can build, and you were trained as a technician. We need some barges and launches in order to get things distributed around the islands. You were successful in recovering that Filipino launch for us. We want you to head-up getting us some boats for water travel."

Lang tried to digest all the Colonel was saying. "Where and when is this going to happen?"

"Port Lamon. There used to be a big commercial sawmill there. A typhoon came through a few months ago and blew everything apart. It looks like a battlefield. However, back in the weeds there is a good supply of lumber. The Japs fly over it all the time and it looks like there is nothing left. They have never gone in to look at it, and they need lumber too. There is a good machine shop, and all the workers still live in the area."

"Where is it located?"

"Down the coast near Hinatuan. Back in a bay area, and pretty well concealed. We need launches, and there is enough material there to do the job. You will have to scrounge motors wherever you can. Your friend Neveling knows the area and can help you."

"Waldo is good with machinery. I'll have to talk him into staying with me. I think he will do it."

"Well, you will be in control. You have been appointed the Commanding Officer of the Port Lamon District, serving under Colonel Childress who is commander of the 107th Division, and Captain Knortz who is regional commander for part of the Surigao District."

"Whew! Commanding officer?"

"Someone has to be in charge. You're the man. The Filipinos will not take orders from a Private First Class, even if you are six foot three. As of July 1, you are a Second Lieutenant in the United States Army."

Lang sat at the table dumfounded. He took a drink of his nearly cold nearly coffee. He took a deep breath, trying to comprehend this new responsibility.

"You will have to hire local labor to get the job done. We have one million pesos (three hundred fifty thousand dollars) for your operation. We'll have to set up some standards, pay levels, and organization. We'll spend a few days working it out. Let's start by putting these bars on you."

Colonel Fertig pinned a gold bar on the coarse fabric of Lang's Filipino-made shirt. Many questions raced through Lang's mind. However, he would have time to sort things out, and he would have to take charge.

After several more days of planning, Dick traveled two weeks back to the east coast to Hinatuan, and south to Port Lamon to assess the situation. With Ernie's help word was spread about that they needed mechanics and woodworkers, and soon signed nearly one hundred workers. Two of the workers were Japanese that had immigrated and become Philippine citizens. They proved to be loyal and hard working members of Lang's crew. The new crews immediately began rebuilding the machine shop. The area could not be cleaned up too well, as it still had to look like a disaster to fool the Japanese. Lang took an inventory of the lumber and found over two million board feet hidden in various locations in Port Lamon.

One of his first visitors was Captain Knortz, a regional commander in Surigao, at the northern tip of Mindanao. The captain was pleased with Lang's promotion and immediately asked for a boat to meet his needs. The captain was constantly dashing about the small islands and traveling back and forth to division headquarters. He needed a small fast boat that could also carry some quantity of material. Captain Knortz was very popular since he had worked with the local Filipinos for several months and earned their respect. He was cheerful and engaging, qualities the Filipinos enjoyed.

Captain Knortz surrendered to the Japanese on Mindanao when the Philippines fell. He was in the prison camp for about two weeks when he managed to escape. Working his way to

Mindanao Island - Port Lamon

northern Mindanao, he was one of the first officers to begin guerrilla warfare. Because of his relationship with the local natives, he became the main troubleshooter in the area. If any of the guerrilla bands got out of hand, he took control of the situation and soon had everyone back in line. He was particularly adept at working with the independent guerrilla groups who wanted to be totally independent. He managed to redirect their energies toward killing their common enemy, and as a result, they inflicted many losses on the Japanese garrisons.

Waldo and Dick immediately went to work on their first boat project. They learned that a hull from a Japanese lumber company launch had been stored in a cove on one of the islands. Lang immediately dispatched a crew of Filipinos to retrieve it. Waldo made a few inquiries, did some searching, and located an unused twenty-five horsepower diesel engine in a nearby village. The Filipino crew went about rebuilding and re-caulking the launch, building a new deck and deckhouse. Steel nails would rust out from exposure to salt water, so one crew of Filipino workers made copper nails from oversized copper electrical wire found on the island. Waldo disassembled the diesel engine, reassembled it after cleaning all the parts, and had it operating in a week.

It took three weeks to complete rebuilding the launch. On the test run the launch ran like new, and cruised at about ten knots per hour. Captain Knortz took command of the vessel and named it "The Albert McCarthy" after an American mestizo who had been killed a few days earlier. The Filipino workers took great pride in honoring one of their own.

Captain Knortz used the Albert McCarthy on his first mission. It was one of the first submarine rendezvous for delivering of supplies on the east coast. Under the cover of night, the two vessels met in amongst the many small islands for concealment. When the transfer of cargo was made and messages exchanged, the ropes were released and the submarine slipped away into the depths. The deck of the Albert McCarthy was piled high with boxes of goods to supply the guerrillas, but on this maiden voyage was overloaded. As they passed between two small islands and into the open sea, the launch suddenly hit high waves that swamped the vessel, capsizing it. As the vessel overturned, several of the crew and Captain Knortz were hit by the falling cargo and drowned. The Albert McCarthy sank in the deep water, and most of the cargo was lost, except for the few cases that washed ashore on nearby islands.

The loss of Knortz and the crew saddened the workers at Port Lamon. The Filipinos dearly loved Captain Knortz. Everyone mourned his death and many prayers were offered in his behalf. They were equally sorry to lose the Albert McCarthy.

Soon after the tragedy Lang and Neveling were summoned to the regimental headquarters near Butuan. They met Captain Marshall, who replaced Knortz as the regional commander. The men spent some time getting acquainted as Lang explained his operation. The Captain then explained the reason they had been called to regimental headquarters. The men were to receive their share of the most recent shipment of supplies that recently arrived from Australia.

Santa Claus had arrived! They received new uniforms, medical supplies including atabrine (for treating malaria), carbine rifles, Tommy guns, shaving equipment, soap, underwear, socks, toothpaste, and toothbrushes. Better yet, Lang received a new pair of 13 EEE jungle boots. These items were non-existent for over two years. It was difficult to describe the feelings of the two men. The ecstasy and delight of each new experience was overwhelming. They tried out their new toothbrushes, brushing for an extended period to feel the wonderful freshness in their mouth. They bathed with real soap, and put on their new khaki uniforms, with a canvass belt. They each had several pair of cotton socks. The jungle boots were a little tight on Dick, but would fit as the footpad shrunk to normal size. The main difficulty was trying to walk in the boots. Walking barefoot for so long, the toes were used to grabbing the soil, and it took some un-learning for several days for the feet to relax. Yes, Santa had come to Mindanao in mid-summer!

When they returned to Port Lamon the Filipinos had the first evidence that supplies were actually being landed by submarine on a monthly basis. They had been suspicious all this time, but now they believed.

Captain Marshall now placed his request. He needed a seaworthy boat capable of making trips anywhere in the islands during the monsoon season. It had to be able to carry a good quantity of supplies with safety and stability. The boat works had manufactured a number of small launches, sixteen to twenty feet long with an eight foot beam, but they proved to be useless during the strong wind and rains of the monsoon season which lasted three or four months a year. Along the east and north coasts of Mindanao, the easterly winds can create very rough seas.

After much discussion, Waldo and Dick decided that a large, strongly built native banca, with a sail and an engine would meet the Captains requirements. They searched the islands and located a native banca that was twenty-six feet long with a ten-foot beam. Waldo managed to find a semi-diesel engine, German-made, that would meet the requirements for a boat that size. They decided that this might be their biggest project, the flagship of their fleet. They rolled up their sleeves and went to work.

They repaired the banca and got it into first class condition. Again, Waldo disassembled the engine and rebuilt it in perfect working order. One of the drive shaft bearings was worn out, and there was no metal available to replace it. One of the Filipino machinists suggested using a very hard wood, and found lumber from a slow growing tree that was very dense. A part was roughed-out, machined to close tolerances, oil hardened, and it proved to work perfectly.

The boat builders learned they might have access to some armament for their boat. Headquarters had a fifty-caliber machine gun and a twenty-millimeter cannon available. They incorporated mountings for the guns in their boat construction.

Dick and Waldo decided some armor plating might be appropriate. They located old saw blades from the sawmill that were almost one-quarter inch thick. The large round blades were permanently mounted on the front, sides and rear of the banca. The saw blades looked unusual, in fact downright funny, but would serve a good purpose if the boat was ever exposed to small arms' fire.

The engine was finally installed and several test runs were made. The banca could move along at about fifteen knots per hour, helped with a full sail in a moderate wind. They had built a first class combat boat that could be used year around in the Mindanao waters.

They named the boat the *"So What."*

Waldo assumed command of the banca and selected ten good fighting men for a crew. He took his crew to division headquarters where they picked up the heavy weapons and fastened them to the deck. They mounted the fifty-caliber machine gun on the port side and the twenty-millimeter cannon on the starboard side. Gun crews were selected and they ran a number of exercises on storage of ammunition and how to use the equipment. The *So What* was now ready to do battle.

About this same time Lieutenant Lang responded to a call from division headquarters. Arriving at headquarters, he signed for and received a radio transmitter and receiver. He received instructions on codes and how to use them. An experienced radio operator was also assigned to him, and Lang was told where to set up the radio operation. Lang's command responsibilities had taken a new turn. He not only was building boats, but he was also in charge of an observation radio station, a dry dock, and a machine shop. For good measure, they assigned him a Filipino lieutenant and a detachment of twenty soldiers with orders to guard Lang's section of the coast.

Port Lamon also had two young sisters living there who produced cigarettes for the workers. They processed the homegrown tobacco, found the paper and worked full time at rolling cigarettes. Liling and Biling Velelos, young girls ages fourteen and fifteen, were very popular with the Filipino workers, and according to Lang, "cuter than a bug's ear."

Liling

Cigarettes were in demand and the young girls efforts were greatly appreciated by all the workers with a cigarette habit, and some workers without a habit.

Ernie Lancen was a very able assistant for Lang, looking after daily tasks and handling special assignments. Ernie was an extremely handsome young man, and usually kept company with a dalaga in every town. In Port Lamon, he was keeping company with an extremely attractive young miss, who was very enamored of Ernie and pursued him daily. In trying to slow down her pursuit and their relationship, Ernie treated her a bit too roughly. She decided to teach Ernie a lesson, and perhaps too possessively, went to the local Magistrate and filed a complaint. The Magistrate called Ernie into his court, redressed him, and sentenced him to two weeks in confinement. After Ernie's second day of confinement the young woman appeared in the Magistrate's court with tearstained eyes, begging the Magistrate to release Ernie, "because he has suffered enough!"

When Lang returned to Port Lamon he became concerned about the quantity of lumber in their possession. If the Japanese found out about it, they would immediately send a substantial force of men to capture it, since they were desperate for lumber. Lang decided to relocate the lumber, and moved it to various hideouts in the interior. They successfully distributed it without detection.

Lang received word that an American woman and her baby were in Hinatuan and needed assistance in avoiding the Japanese. Glenda Kritzer was traveling with her two-year old child, and had worked her way up the coast from Davao. Her husband worked for a stevedoring company in Davao, was captured by the Japanese, and made to work in the Davao harbor. Lang brought her to Port Lamon where she would be safe, then made arrangements to get her aboard a submarine bound for Australia. The final arrangements were made, and two weeks later Glenda and her son were able to leave Mindanao.

Lang now felt a great responsibility toward his new radio station. It was located in the hills with good visibility of the coast in both directions. The antenna was carefully strung between the coconut trees to avoid detection, and a small hut was constructed to keep the radio equipment out of the weather. Several escape routes were established, in case Japanese squads wandering about in the hills got too close.

Lang's boat operation was well organized, with Filipino's in responsible management positions. Lang could now concentrate on spying on Japanese shipping, reporting all boat, plane, and Japanese troop movements along the northeast coast to the SOUWESPAC headquarters.

So What

Chapter Eleven

THE NAVAL BATTLE

Lang traveled between his lookout station and the machine shop on a regular basis, making certain his operations were continuing as he intended. Early in his training on the islands, one of his commanding officers gave him some friendly advice that he found to be true. "Make friends with the natives!" Dick learned that the Filipino's sense of family meant everything. It developed a profound sense of belonging, and built family solidarity. As a result it deprived the individual of some measure of privacy, providing little opportunity for self-development. The individual was little or nothing in oneself, but a cog in the family machine. Any strong expression of individuality was discouraged, and conformity to the family concept was enforced. It fostered the durability and strength of the Filipinos. They were attentive, true to their family, and tried to do their best. They were friendly and outgoing, not at all secretive. Everyone's business was everyone else's business. There were no secrets. Some of these qualities Lang understood and appreciated. They included certain elements of the lifestyle of a young Catholic boy growing up in Haverhill IA.

Waldo Neveling entered into being a ship's captain with enthusiasm. He made many trips along the coast delivering supplies to guerrilla installations. As a result he became familiar with the smaller islands up and down the coast and how to use them for protection during passage through Japanese held territory. The *So What* was performing up to expectations, and his chosen crew was dedicated in carrying out their responsibilities. He had several near confrontations with the Japanese, but always managed to avoid direct conflict with them.

In February 1944, Waldo went to division headquarters to pick up a load of supplies. Division headquarters moved periodically in order to avoid confrontations with the enemy, which was constantly on the prowl to find them. On this date, division HQ was located five miles from the coast, up the Tago River.

Waldo entered the river, proceeding rather boldly into the interior. When he was about two miles up the river, he and the crew heard a few rifle shots that echoed down the river. Thinking it was guerrillas taking target practice, they continued up stream. Waldo was displaying the American flag so as not to be mistaken for the enemy by guerrillas eager to pick-off unsuspecting Japanese crewmembers. A small boy ran to the river's edge shouting, "Daghan hoppoon tass sa subig! Daghan hoppoon tass sa subig!" Translated into English, the young boy was saying, "There are many Japanese up the river!" The lad recognized the boat flying the American flag and immediately called out with the warning.

The previous day the Japanese had located the guerrilla division headquarters and attacked it with a large contingent of soldiers. The Japanese worked inland and were being repelled by the guerrillas, but the fighting continued for over a month with attack and counter attack. The Japanese never did capture the division headquarters, and finally withdrew after experiencing heavy losses.

Waldo responded to the young lad's warning, and turned his banca about, as he did not want to be trapped in a narrow river. He managed to leave the mouth of the river; proceeding to a small port purported to be in guerrilla hands. As the *So What* entered the port, they spotted two Japanese naval craft close to shore. Again, Waldo swung his boat about, hoping to sneak out of the port without being noticed by the Japanese naval craft. Completing the turn, he discovered the banca was heading straight for a Japanese cargo boat approaching the bay.

Waldo was forced to go near the shore on his escape route, so he decided to secure what he was carrying. He directed half of the crew to wade ashore, carrying their secret orders, maps and the most valuable supplies. The men scrambled up the beach into the jungle, and looked for a secure defensible location. Waldo decided it was time to confront the enemy, and he turned his banca straight at the freighter. He ordered the gunner at the twenty-millimeter gun to spray the deck of the Japanese boat, hoping to hit the crew and the bridge. Taking the machine gun fire the freighter turned out to sea, but responded to the firing with their three or four inch cannon. When several cannon shots raised waterspouts close by, Waldo left the confrontation, trying to get out to sea away from the freighter. The freighter turned to chase the *So What*. Waldo responded with several bursts from the twenty-millimeter cannon and knocked down one of the masts on the Japanese boat. The freighter turned from the confrontation and headed into the port area.

Turning back to sea Waldo decided the safest place to hide was Port Lamon, and charted a course through the islands in that general direction. They retrieved the men from shore and headed home.

One of the crew suddenly shouted, "Listen!" They could detect an airplane motor in the distance, and suddenly a Japanese float-plane dropped from the clouds above, making a pass over the *So What*. Fortunately, the plane did not immediately recognize them as an enemy until it turned for another pass. The gunners on the *So What* were ready. As the plane bore down on them, firing its thirty caliber machine guns, the Filipino gunners opened fire with the twenty and the fifty. Smoke poured from the engine, as it passed over the banca; the plane's motor continued to sputter for another minute, whereupon it crashed into the open sea with a tremendous spout of water. The men cheered as they recorded their first airplane shot down.

As they turned on their homeward course, the wind picked up causing rough seas. Waldo sought a route that might reduce exposure to the wind and rough seas. Changing course they were suddenly exposed to two Japanese launches, each carrying ten to twelve soldiers. The launches were some distance apart, but also fighting the wind and rough seas. The Japanese soldiers were armed with rifles and a light thirty-caliber machine gun. One launch immediately opened fire, although out of range, trying to hit the banca below the water line. Fortunately, the saw blades mounted on the side of the *So What* did their work, deflecting the lighter shells. The gunner manning the twenty-millimeter cannon had difficulty taking aim because of the rough seas, but waited patiently until he was rocking with the boat, and delivered a burst which killed a number of Japanese in the boat, but most important-ly opened large gaping holes in the launch at the water line. The launch slowly lowered in the water, with the aft finally lifting ver-tically as the vessel slipped beneath the waves. The seas were too rough, and distance too great, to determine if any of the soldiers were swimming away. The Filipinos would have liked to pick them off with rifles while they were in the water, but Waldo had other worries on his mind.

The second launch had turned and was approaching them head on. It made a very small target. The small arms' fire was still too far away to be accurate, but the fifty-caliber machine gun was now ready to do its part. The gunner waited until the heavy seas lifted the prow of the launch to its highest point. The Filipino gave it a five-second burst, throwing two hundred fifty one-half inch pieces of metal at the prow. A jagged hole appeared in the prow of the launch, and as the launch nosed down, a burst raked the deck. Another burst caught the aft steering control. The launch bobbed once and disappeared. There were no survivors.

The men cheered at the success of the machine gunners, and clapped each other on the back. They had four close encounters in succession, with no losses. The armor plate on the *So What* had saved them from possible sinking. Waldo had trained them well, and they were cool under fire.

They set a course for Port Lamon, keeping a watchful eye for any other unexpected interruptions. When they reached Port Lamon they told their story and a crowd gathered, so they told it again, and again, and again. Lang decided it was time for a celebration, and purchased several containers of tuba. As at most Filipino social events, they roasted a pig and had a royal celebration. They had fought off an armed freighter. They had shot down a seaplane, sunk two launches and killed twenty-plus Japanese soldiers that were probably reinforcing the soldiers fighting up the Tago River. The celebration lasted late into the evening, until the tuba was all gone. After all, the tuba has to be consumed because it turns sour after a week.

Tuba was the main alcoholic drink of the Filipinos, because of its easy access. It is the fermented sap collected near the top of palm trees. During certain seasons the sap is forced out of the tree by internal pressure, and once exposed to air starts the fermenting process. Bands of monkeys are known to identify these trees, and Filipinos report seeing a number of monkeys acting in a suspiciously human manner when they have consumed too much tuba.

Lang continued to spend time at the lookout point, traveling down to Port Lamon every few days. Captain Oliver, a former schoolteacher, who had become good friends with Dick, visited Lang in his camp. Since Lang was now dealing with other members of headquarters, he met many more officers who had specific duties in Colonel Fertig's 10th Army. Captain Oliver was working with radio installations, and wanted to inspect Lang's installation above Port Lamon.

Oliver and Lang were sitting in the observation post one afternoon, when Oliver mentioned that he had to use the bathroom. He proceeded to pick up his necessary supplies and headed into the bush to relieve himself. Suddenly Lang heard a pistol shot. Thinking a Japanese patrol might have succeeded in slipping in behind them, Lang grabbed his carbine and headed up the path. Captain Oliver stepped out of the bush. Draped over his shoulders was a very big python snake. The head was dragging on the ground on one side and the tail was dragging along the ground on the other side. Oliver casually said, "I think I just caught dinner for tonight."

It actually served the radio crew for several nights. It seems that python has no integral fat, so it cannot be fried without some

sort of grease. However, Ernie was an excellent cook and he prepared the python Filipino style. Cut into steak-sized pieces and
boiled in coconut milk until it is soft, it becomes a real delicacy. It
seems that snake, like monkey and unusual jungle rodents, when
properly cooked tastes "just like chicken." Since the python snakes
are usually found along stream and river bottoms, Lang often
referred to the meat as "Anahowan Ground Steak."

Lang was meeting with a crew chief at the boat works, discussing some boat construction details, when a young Filipino ran
up to him. "Mr. Lang! Mr. Lang. Come quick. Man shot! Man
shot!" Lang ran down to the beach where a young Filipino was
lying in a banca, bleeding from a wound.

A group of Filipino fisherman were out on a coral reef throwing
their fly-nets, used for trapping fish in shallow water. A Japanese
launch motored by carrying ten or twelve soldiers. One soldier
suddenly raised his rifle and shot the fisherman in an unprovoked
act. The bullet entered his neck muscle, knocking him out of the
boat. His friends pulled him back into the banca and paddled as
fast as they could for Port Lamon.

Lang assessed the situation and said, "He is hit pretty bad
and has lost a lot of blood. I don't think I can help him. Is there a
doctor in Hinatuan?"

The boy was pleading. "He no live to Hinatuan. You lieutenant! You must help him!" The others chimed in. "You help!
You Help!"

Lang took the wounded fisherman to the boat works where
they had a medical kit that was included in a submarine supply
delivery. Lang cleaned the wound with water, and then swabbed it
out with hydrogen peroxide. The kit contained a pair of long
nosed forceps. After dipping them in hydrogen peroxide, he gingerly entered the wound. The fisherman was very silent and stoic,
as Lang did not have any thing to kill the pain. Lang gingerly
probed the wound and felt a hard object. He managed to grasp the
bullet deep in the wound with the forceps and slowly withdrew it.
Again, he cleansed the wound with hydrogen peroxide, sprinkled
it with sulfa powder, and applied a bandage. Giving the fisherman

several sulfa-thiozol tablets, he sent him home under the care of several Filipino fishermen. Lang was concerned about infection and particularly the numerous infectious diseases that thrive in the warm, moist Philippine climate.

Two weeks later the wounded fisherman returned to Port Lamon and brought Lang two chickens in payment for saving his life. Lang was embarrassed to accept the chickens, but to not accept them would have been an insult.

Lang still has the forceps today as a memento of the event. He considers them very valuable. They are worth, at the very least, two chickens.

News of Lang's success in removing the bullet was quietly broadcast throughout the Filipino community. Soon Lang was contacted to treat a number of accidents and miscellaneous pains. The most serious accident was another fisherman who appeared at his door one day with an arrow through his arm. The Filipino fisherman fashioned a hollow bamboo tube with a rubber band and would walk through the shallow water shooting fish with their makeshift tube slingshot. This unfortunate fisherman was hit with an arrow on a glancing blow, piercing his arm but missing the arm bones.

The handmade arrows were barbed on the side near the head so fish could not wriggle out of the arrow when hit. Lang laid the arm and arrow on a solid table, and used his bolo knife to cut the arrow in two, close to the fisherman's arm. Then he gingerly pulled the shortened arrow through the arm being careful not to increase the size of the wound. Again, he treated the wound as he had previously, and the fisherman left happy.

The fisherman did not return with chickens, but Ernie never ran out of fish when preparing meals for Lieutenant Lang.

Lang constantly tried to get word back to his family that he was safe. However, it was difficult to get messages through, as headquarters did not want the Japanese to find out where or who the Americans were. One of Lang's officer acquaintances left the island by submarine, and shipped back to the United States. He wrote Anna Lang the letter, informing her "I have seen Dick Lang.

He is alive and well. I cannot tell you where he is located."

About this same time Mr. and Mrs. Lang were contacted by a gentleman from the War Department, who asked them to meet him in Marshalltown. First, the representative swore them to absolute secrecy. They could not tell other members of the family, minister, or friends. Then the war department representative passed on the message. "Your son Dick Lang is alive and well. He is still in the Philippine Islands but I cannot tell you his exact location."

The word from two different sources stating Dick was alive and well was a great relief for the Lang family.

Margaret continued to write Dick three times a week, dutifully sending the letters to the War Department in Washington D.C. They refused to deliver the letters, again because if they accidentally fell into enemy hands, they might expose the numbers and location of the guerrillas. Margaret read an article in the Reader's Digest that a number of soldiers had taken to the hills in the Philippine Islands and were living on a pineapple plantation. They did not have any names or locations, but mentioned that they were continuing the war effort by scouting and fighting the Japanese. This gave great encouragement to Margaret, who had a map of the Philippine Islands with the Del Monte plantation clearly identified on Mindanao. Margaret's last letter received by Dick was while he was stationed at Clark Field, Luzon, in late November 1941. Margaret's last letter from Dick was about that same time.

Lang was working at the radio outpost one noon when a Filipino soldier approached and handed him a letter. It was a letter from Margaret. Included was a recent picture, taken in a studio in Des Moines. Lang took the letter up the path, into the jungle, sat down on a fallen coconut log and read the letter, and reread the letter several times. Then he broke down and sobbed "like a baby" for a half-hour.

Chapter Twelve

RETREAT

After Waldo's successful naval engagement and the big party, and once the heads had stopped throbbing, things returned to normal at Port Lamon. Normal, except that *So What's* success against the Japanese alerted them to a growing problem of resistance. A few days later the Japanese initiated an air search, patrolling the coast to find concentrations of native boats, and particularly big boats like the *So What*.

Exposure to rough weather had not been kind to the big banca, and although it performed well, it took quite a beating. Lang and Neveling decided to put it into dry dock for repairs. Workers excavated a section of the beach where the boat could be winched to high ground, and propped it in the air so the entire under-structure could be inspected and repaired. Even though partially concealed by trees, the *So What* was still big enough to spot from the air.

A few days later Japanese search planes filled the air, patrolling up and down the coastline. Search planes apparently located the *So What*, but the planes left the site without firing a shot. That evening about six o'clock, a lone Japanese twin-engine bomber swooped over the hills heading directly for the large boat, flying about five hundred feet high. Waldo just happened to be standing on the deck of the *So What*, and raced to the twenty-millimeter cannon. As the plane approached within range Waldo let fly with a four-second burst, scoring several hits. The plane immediately banked to the left, which exposed the entire underside of the airplane. As it turned Waldo gave it another burst, and tracer bullets were seen flying through the fuselage and tail section. The plane left without firing a shot or dropping a bomb, heading out to sea.

Lank knew that if it made it back to its base, the Japanese would return with an armada, and devastate the area. Lang and Waldo decided to relocate the two big guns. The guns were removed from the baroto and one was mounted at each end of the port dock. This would give more firepower, and permit covering a larger firing area.

The Filipinos were up the next morning, setting up a defense system, distributing ammunition, and preparing their weapons for an anticipated battle. As they worked, word was received from the native grapevine that the Japanese bomber had managed to fly about ten miles, when it crashed on the coast near the beach in Hinatuan Bay. The crew had escaped injury, taken a machine gun from the plane, and set up a defense perimeter against the guerrillas on shore. Lang decided to check out the situation. He took three of his soldiers, a gun crew, and the fifty-caliber machine gun mounted on a large baroto and headed up the coast. They arrived about dusk, and waited until it was almost dark. The bomber made a safe belly landing, and they found it lying on rocks near the shore, with the waves lapping the underside of the plane. Edging into shore, Lang deployed three men in a circle to contain the Japanese crew, then settled in for the night. At dawn, he sent two men ashore as scouts to determine the situation. They returned with the news that the Japanese crew had found a small baroto and were preparing to leave the island. The flight crew was within shooting range, and a Filipino Guerrilla scored a hit knocking one Japanese airman out of the boat. The other four Japanese pushed off and started paddling frantically to get out of rifle range. Lang sent a runner down the beach to alert guerrillas in the area to be aware of the fleeing Japanese. The baroto was some distance offshore, but the guerrillas kept them under observation as they made their way south around the island. Lang later learned that the plane's crew had paddled a good distance south, but ran into rough water. Their small baroto capsized, and the air crew swam towards the shore. As they were wading inland, the guerrillas easily eliminated them one at a time.

Lang assembled his men and inspected the airplane, salvaging all useful equipment. It was a real find. There were air charts of all the local islands on the coast. The biggest bonus by far, was three small machine guns, and two twenty-millimeter guns with lots of ammunition. Fifty-caliber machine guns fired a projectile one-half inch in diameter, with good power. The twenty-millimeter projectile was eight/tenths of an inch in diameter, with a bigger firing charge. It could do a good deal of damage in a shorter time. Since both guns fired three thousand rounds per minute, it meant a one second burst would hurl fifty projectiles in the general vicinity of a target. It provided a much better defense against boats and airplanes. With the anticipated activity from the Japanese, these weapons would be most valuable.

The guerrillas salvaged the radio equipment, miscellaneous controls, wire, switches and all other items that could be used somehow, somewhere. The twenty-millimeter guns were by far the most important acquisition. They would be put to good use soon enough.

The American military forces were now "island-hopping" their way across the south Pacific. Instead of taking each island in sequence, which would have been costly in terms of life and equipment, they went after strategic islands where airfields could be quickly constructed or repaired. Once the airfields were in place the islands in between could be bombed and harassed, forcing the Japanese to withdraw or be starved into submission. Most Japanese followed the "bushida code," fighting to their death. Many of the in-between islands were evacuated by the Japanese under the cover of night and the fighting men relocated to islands closer to Japan.

The Japanese realized that the Philippine Islands were necessary for the defense of their home island, and decided to make a stand there. The rocky, jungle covered islands favored a defensive fighting strategy. America would pay a high price to invade and retake control of the Philippine Islands.

The Japanese began bringing more and more troops to the islands. Mindanao had many Japanese troops on the south, west, and north shores of Mindanao. Soon they would reinforce the troops on the eastern side of the island. Every day Lang's radio team observed convoys of Japanese ships moving up and down the coast. All sightings were immediately reported to the headquarters of the Southwest Pacific, which assessed the information from all other observation posts. The naval task forces were playing cat-and-mouse games with the rebuilt Japanese navy, and soon there would be a major confrontation somewhere near the Philippine Islands.

The convoys became prime targets for American planes and submarines. Each day there would be a loud explosion and smoke on the horizon. The fighting remains of the Japanese navy, the big ships, periodically moved through the area, trying to draw the U.S. Navy into a big sea battle. America had been successful in sinking a major portion of the Japanese aircraft carrier fleet, but was avoiding confrontation with the Japanese main force, choosing to fight them when the U.S. Navy had an advantage. In the meantime, the submarines continued to harass Japanese shipping.

Early on the morning of April 28, 1944, three small Japanese transports and three landing barges slowly passed by the observation point, moving south. Lang observed them with his binoculars as they anchored off Hinatuan Bay. The barges pulled alongside the transports, loaded the soldiers, and started toward shore. There were only a few guerrillas stationed in Hinatuan, and they were not able to offer any opposition. The Japanese landed with very little difficulty. Lang watched as the landing barges returned to the transports, picked up another load of soldiers, and set a course for Port Lamon.

When Lang first spotted the transports, he ordered everything he did not want the Japanese to get to be relocated and hidden in the hills. He alerted the Filipino citizens so they could pack their essentials and move to the hills. The radio operator, notified of the impending attack, packed his equipment and moved to a new location further into the hills. The residents knew this day would come, and had been preparing for it. The retreat was orderly, and most people managed to save those items that were important to them. They moved to camps in the hills, built for just this situation. Food and ammunition were concealed in a series of camps up the mountainside.

Waldo had been hurt in a fall and was mending, so two Filipinos helped to move him into the hills.

Lang had only ten soldiers with him, and had another twenty-three deployed along the beach in strategic locations. They decided to take a stand and do as much damage as they could before retiring into the hills. As the barges of Japanese troops neared the shore, the transports opened with a volley of three and four inch cannons spraying the beach. As the barges got closer to the beach, the Filipinos opened with small arms fire, inflicting some damage. It was difficult to slow down the incoming Japanese without mortars or artillery to stop the barges or pin down the infantry. The Filipinos were out numbered twenty to one, and it was obvious their defense was useless. Lang called his troops in, and they retreated to the hills, without loss of life, or injury.

The Japanese landed and secured a beachhead before sending patrols inland. About forty soldiers moved immediately up the hills, headed for the radio station. They obviously knew its' location, taking the shortest path right to it. When they arrived at the observation point, they found an empty, decrepit hut, and no equipment.

The radio operator had hidden the radio so cleverly; it took Lang two days to track him down. They immediately strung an antenna and notified Pacific Headquarters.

The Japanese left two hundred men each in Hinataun and Port Lamon. They far outnumbered the guerrillas, and had more fire-power. Lang decided the best fight was to wait until they sent a patrol into the mountains and ambush them along the trails. The guerrillas would institute a hit-and-run war as the Japanese patrols ventured deeper into the jungle. The local Filipinos were in the mountains and not subject to the personal atrocities committed to make them reveal the whereabouts of the guerrillas.

Once Waldo was better and able to get around, they planned several surprise attacks to harass the Japanese in their housing. Late one evening Lang took all of his men and several machine guns into the Japanese area. They positioned the guerrillas on two adjoining sides of the barracks where the Japanese soldiers were sleeping, arranging the men so the Filipinos would not be firing into each other. The plan was to deliver a fulisade of heavy fire-power for a short period of time, then retreat while the Japanese were recovering. At the agreed time Lang gave the command to fire and the Filipinos emptied their weapons into the building. As the firing by the Filipinos stopped, the men melted back into the forest. The Japanese hastily retrieved their weapons, and fired into the darkness. There were no casualties in the guerrilla ranks.

Lang later learned that a small number of the Japanese were killed and several wounded. The raid had been a success, but had not produced the casualties they had intended. They would now have to find different ways to fight the invaders. The Japanese would not take the guerrillas hit-and-run tactics lightly.

Chapter Thirteen

TRAPPED

Lang decided to continue "bothering" the Japanese garrison stationed in Port Lamon, hoping to keep them from moving inland. It was obvious the Japanese wanted to control the shores and keep Americans from invading. Mindanao was a large island, with several airfields. If the Americans controlled those airfields, many of the surrounding islands would be indefensible. Colonel Fertig already had several secret airfields spotted around the island, and they might be the main thrust of the new Japanese landings.

Lang felt more secure with his troops, now that they had received aid from SOUWESPAC. With carbines, Tommy guns, and Garand rifles, they had considerably more firepower. They also had plenty of ammunition, so they were not handing out ten shells to each soldier and telling the men to make every round count. In addition, Lang had quantities of ammunition deposited at a number of sites in the interior, so if the men did retreat, they had something to fight back with. They were now entering a new phase of guerrilla warfare.

Two or three days after hitting the barracks Lang decided to hit them once again. The area between the village and the jungle was covered with coogan grass, three to four feet high with isolated areas six to eight feet high. It varied in width from three hundred feet to a quarter of a mile. It was good cover, enabling the guerrillas to sneak close to the village and observe the activities of the

Japanese. Areas of it were very thick, making it difficult to walk through. Other areas thinned out, making it possible to run in it.

Lang selected Ernie and three of his men for a hit-and-run action. They crawled to within four hundred feet of the barracks, where they could see soldiers assembling and moving about. They decided to wait until a patrol was assembled, ambush them with automatic weapons, then run for the hills before other soldiers could organize a pursuit team. As they positioned themselves for a good field of fire, they heard a rustling. A patrol was already out, and there were twenty Japanese soldiers standing only fifty feet behind them.

Ernie Lancen, who was carrying a Tommy gun, spun around and started giving them short bursts. Lang and the other men were carrying semi-automatic carbines. Flipping the lever to automatic, they started to spray the area with thirty caliber bullets. A brief fire-fight ensued with the Japanese, who were even more surprised, firing back with their rifles.

Suddenly, Lang's three guerrillas made a dash for the taller grass, running as fast as they could, as low as they could. Lang and Ernie continued to spray the area in short bursts. Ernie decided he did not like the odds, and also bolted for the denser grass stopping once or twice to fire back.

Lang was in a quandary. At six foot three, he would make a much larger target. He decided he could not run too far in an open field without covering fire as they might get a bead on him. He ran a short distance, then kneeling, stopped to fire his carbine. He repeated this action twice more, and then dove into the weeds. Crab crawling a short distance, he found denser grass that leaned in all directions and slid under trying not to move the grass above. He stretched out with his weapon overhead in case he would have to come out firing. Laying on his back, he slipped his .45 automatic out of the holster, in case he needed a short shot through the heavy grass.

The Japanese soldiers who were still mobile organized a search. Three soldiers had been killed and four were wounded. One stayed with the wounded, and the remaining twelve began to search the area. At first, the Japanese soldiers were nervous, firing at any grass moved by the breeze. They fixed their bayonets, stabbing at every clump of grass and depression in the ground. One soldier approached Lang's position slashing the fallen coogan grass, but not stabbing the ground. Lang watched the shiny bayonet swing overhead, reflecting sunlight off his wristwatch. He was sweating profusely, and a few ants and beetles in the area were crawling up his arms and neck. He considered pulling his arm up to take the Jap out, but he knew the tangled grass would not let him move quickly. The Japanese soldier moved slowly on, breathing heavily, turning and slashing every few steps. The Japanese were now working their way in the direction the guerrillas had run, with their back to Lang. Lang began to inch his way at an oblique angle, and after moving fifty feet, found a small ravine where he could avoid detection. His body just fit the ravine, but there was room to move without disturbing the grass. It seemed secure enough, and he waited there until dark.

Lang listened to the noises of the area, the birds chattering, insects buzzing, and coogan grass blowing in the wind. The Japanese had moved some distance away, but Lang suspected they might circle back. The short, stocky, Japanese had difficulty seeing over parts of the grass grown very tall. Lang was very thirsty, but did not want to risk pulling out his canteen for a drink. He thought about how his assignment had changed. His Filipino crews had successfully built several barotos for inter-island travel. His radio observation post had moved further and further into the interior of the island. He was now an infantry officer, since the Japanese now occupied Port Lamon. If he got back to headquarters safely, he would have to start planning new strategies. If he was killed in this ravine, how would Margaret find out about it? He thought about the ten-day honeymoon in Albuquerque, and wondered if that was the last time he would see Margaret. He wondered if Margaret knew he was alive. Why are the birds quiet? He slowly raised his head and strained to peer through the thick grass.

Late afternoon the Japanese soldiers returned to their comrades, and carried them back to the village and the garrison. They moved very cautiously with the trailing soldier walking backward, not wanting to be picked off as they returned.

Lang watched the sun drop behind the jungle trees, and long shadows extended across the tall grass. New sounds were emanating from the jungle, indicating no human activity was in the area. Apparently, the Japanese were not coming back. When it was finally dark, Lang moved through the tall grass, looking for signs of his trail back into the jungle.

Ernie and the three guerrillas made it back to the temporary headquarters and joined the other guerrillas. They excitedly told their story, and were questioned why they had not covered an opportunity for Lang to escape. The men explained they were outnumbered six to one, and did not stop to look back. Waldo and the men assumed Lang was dead, because they heard random shooting by Japanese soldiers after the guerrillas left. The story of Lang's demise was already being spread through the other camps.

It was well after dark when Lang passed through the night lookouts, and walked into the headquarters area. His first words were, "Is there anything left to eat?" The guerrillas gathered around and patted him on the back. Waldo appeared and gave him a long, strong hug. Ernie and the boys recounted there trip back, and felt badly they had left Lang by himself. Lang acknowledged that things did not look good for a while, but remembered that they had killed three Japs, and put several more out of commission. The day had not been a total loss.

Lang and Waldo continued to stay in the area, taking small raiding parties to snipe at the Japanese patrols. After a month of hit-and-run, the two leaders decided they were not doing much good. The more Japanese they killed, the more reinforcements were delivered to the island. The small guerrilla group, now outnumbered by a substantial margin, recognized a major push by the Japanese would easily overrun them. Lang made the decision to join forces with a larger body of guerrillas, and turned his forces over to another commander.

Lang remembered a radio that was stored in a maintenance building in their machine shop area. They would need the radio for further operations as they moved inland. It would involve slipping through Japanese lines into the occupied area, getting the radio and then slipping through the lines again. There was the risk of discovery, and capture would be horrendous. Taken alive, Lang would be tortured beyond the usual inhuman devices in order to learn all they could about the guerrilla forces. Lang was well known to the Japanese, and they would take great delight in his interrogation. There were many stories of how the Japanese treated their prisoners. First Sergeant Talbe was in a prison camp on Luzon, and managed to escape two times. The second capture resulted in being suspended by his thumbs, and a hose placed up his nose at full pressure, a version of the old Chinese water treatment. Sergeant Talbe managed to survive and released when the Americans freed the prison camp. Other prison treatment by the Japanese included a red-hot iron rod applied to various parts of the body. The end treatment was being either bayoneted, disemboweled, or emasculated. Dying would be a welcome relief.

Lang decided to retrieve the radio, and selected his best soldier, Ernie, to accompany him. Late in the afternoon, they left headquarters down a jungle trail toward Port Lamon. They traveled light, carrying only their forty-five sidearm, a bolo knife, a Tommy gun and a backpack large enough to carry the radio. They left behind their canteens and medical packs.

The two men proceeded down the trail at dusk. As they neared the edge of the heavy growth of the jungle, they were aware of voices on the trail behind them. They slipped down an embankment, laying face down with their Tommy guns beside them. A Japanese patrol was stumbling down the trail, having searched the jungle for most of the day. They were anxious to get back for their evening meal, and chatted in their nasal sing–song language, uttering an occasional guttural profanity. The guerrillas could see the soldiers' leg wrappings in the dim light, as they moved by. How many more patrols were out? Usually the Japanese were back in their barracks this time of day. Was it a late patrol? The two guerrillas waited until the patrol was a hundred yards down the trail, then slipped out and followed them. The patrol would identify where the lookout guards were posted, so the guerrillas would not stumble into them in the dark.

They heard the challenge and the response, and moved in a circular path around the guard. Slipping through the coogan grass, they reached the first of the buildings in the lumberyard storage area. Moving cautiously from building shadow to building shadow, Lang and Ernie watched the Japanese move about their camp. The few outdoor lights did little to light the area. Most lights were around the buildings used for barracks and the mess hall. A detail of four soldiers walked past the guerrillas' hiding spot returning from a cleanup task, obviously distressed at their dirty job.

Reaching a small storage building, Ernie deftly lifted the metal latch, swinging the door open just enough to slide in. Empty crates and barrels were in disarray. Hidden inside one of the 'empty' crates, wrapped in a black rubberized sheet and twine, was their radio. Ernie felt his way through the debris, not making a sound. He rotated a wooden crate, carefully setting aside any box that might interfere. When he felt the smooth material and twine, he carefully slid it forward. Lang removed his backpack, and opened the canvas cover. Ernie quietly slipped the package into the backpack, and Lang fed the holding straps through the metal buckle. As Lang swung the pack over his shoulder and put his left arm through, he hit several shovels that were leaning against the doorframe, which fell against a steel barrel. Ernie and Lang held their breath. They heard soldiers running their way. The soldiers entered the building next door, and their flashlights searched through the debris. Lang slipped out the door, with Ernie close behind.

Instead of heading for the coogan grass, they moved into an area where several broken-down trucks were rusting away. The Japanese soldiers moved into the building the guerrillas had just vacated and kicked the empty crates. Once the soldiers were inside the building, Lang and Ernie ran into the coogan grass. Running low, they left the grass and entered the jungle. There was more Japanese activity as the posted guards were reinforced with several other soldiers, who moved about with flashlights looking for signs of trespass. In the black of the night it was impossible to see very far, but Ernie found a path, different from the one they had used to enter the compound. They cautiously made their way into the jungle. When they had traveled far enough to feel they were well out of range of discovery by the Japanese, they found a good spot to rest under a cluster of pandanas plants. Dozing off, they slept until dawn, when they successfully returned to the headquarters compound proudly displaying the recovered radio.

The guerrillas were already packing for a move further inland. Two close calls indicated to Lang the Japanese were getting more active in their pursuit of the guerrillas. With the Americans capturing islands close to the Philippines, perhaps the Japanese were starting to panic. How long would it be until an American invasion fleet would appear on the horizon, and planes began to bomb enemy installations?

Certainly General MacArthur was anxious to return.

General Douglas MacArthur was dearly loved by the Philippine people. An acknowledged military hero, his defense of the Philippine Islands lacked the use of reconnaissance and air cover, and as a result, the Japanese forces succeeded in taking the islands. When he returned, he was welcomed back to the islands as a hero by the Philippine citizens.

Chapter Fourteen

"I SHALL RETURN"

The Japanese continued to reinforce the Port Lamon area, as well as other areas up and down the coast. Trying to reach the coast for supplies meant passing through several Japanese lines of defense, and became quite hazardous. The coast of Mindanao is dotted with small islands, providing concealment for submarines delivering supplies to the guerrillas. With numerous Japanese patrols out every day, the guerrillas still managed to somehow get supplies inland without capture. Every package of candy bars and cigarettes the guerrillas received carried a sticker proclaiming, "I shall return! General Douglas MacArthur." Because the Americans were now capturing islands closer to the Philippines, the Filipinos were encouraged that the Americans soon would be invading their home islands.

Due to the build-up of Japanese forces, Lang and the other officers decided to move the larger band of guerrillas inland to defend the main trails into the interior. Within a week, the Japanese started a new offensive against the guerrillas and immediately attacked the headquarters' location. Fortunately, since the headquarters moved a week earlier, Japanese found nothing but guerrillas hiding in the jungle who put up a ferocious defense. They were like jungle hornets, stinging the Japanese at every hill and in every valley. The Japanese withdrew and cut a new trail into the jungle in an attempt to trap the guerrillas, but they were no better off. The Filipinos used the jungle to their best advantage, and the Japanese paid a heavy toll for their efforts, losing hundreds of men.

The Americans were currently on the Palau Islands, only a few hundred miles from Mindanao. The U.S. Navy was now in Philippine waters on a regular basis threatening the supply routes of the Japanese.

The Japanese staff realized that protecting Mindanao did not have much of a military advantage, and decided to evacuate their troops for a more effective defense of Japan. A fleet of ships arrived to move the men and equipment from the northeast coast of Surigao to Davao, further south. The island observers reported to SOUWESPAC that thirty cargo boats and twenty-two smaller vessels were leaving Surigao for Davao. A day or so later, the Japanese convoy was visited by carrier planes of the U.S. Navy, who proceeded to sink all fifty-two vessels. Some of the boats sunk in shallow water. Larger boats gave up their cargo which subsequently washed up on the Mindanao coast.

Lang was assigned to be in charge of the salvage operation to pick up all the usable cargo in the water and on the beach. Using barotos they had constructed in their machine shop and boat works, Lang's crew traveled the coast visiting sunken ships, recovering salvageable items. The Japanese had stripped the villages of everything useful. Lang's crew recovered clothing, soap, mess kits, uniforms, shoes, and many other items to equip the guerrillas. A most important recovery was numerous barrels of oil that would keep their engines running for many months.

The most important item missing was food. The Japanese had stripped the countryside of everything edible in order to provide for the troops at their new location. The natives and guerrillas were now facing starvation. Their first options were to eat fish, green bananas, and coconuts. They ate "camote in kahoy" (sweet potato in the wood), a tough tree root that was cut in sections and cooked. The interior pulp consisted mostly of starch. The Japanese had harvested all of the camote or sweet potatoes, which were lost when the ships sank. The guerrillas also ate monkey, snakes, beetles, lizards, and grasshoppers. Lang had no problems sitting down to a meal of the new diet forced upon him. He did have difficulty eating grasshoppers, and never did like or get used to them. Nevertheless, he ate them when there was nothing else available.

After the salvage crew transported the usable items to headquarters, Lang once again was assigned to maintain the division radio station. He was pleased to be working alongside the Filipino operator first assigned to him. Lang spent time coding and decoding messages to SOUWESPAC. Most of the messages reported Japanese air activity. This told General MacArthur's headquarters where there were concentrations of aircraft in airfields, which were usually bombed by American aircraft within a few days. Lang continued operating the radio installation for several weeks.

On October 14, 1944, the American forces invaded the east coast of Leyte, the next major island north of Mindanao. General Douglas MacArthur made an appearance in late October, wading through the surf to inform the citizens of the Philippine Islands that true to his word, he did return. General MacArthur issued a press release about the first week of November, 1944, that the fighting was essentially over, and the American soldiers were involved in "mopping-up exercises." In reality, there were still 27,000 Japanese in the hills of Leyte fighting a fierce defensive action. By the end of December most of the major opposition on Leyte was defeated after intense fighting.

Entering the jungle

During those two months, the "mopping up exercise" cost Americans many casualties, because true to their Bushida code, only a handful of Japanese troops surrendered.

Lang continued to operate his radio station, until November, when he received orders to proceed to the north coast of Mindanao to oversee the repair of an airstrip for use in support of the fighting in Leyte. Lang packed his gear, and once more he and Ernie walked to the north coast. Lang organized the local Filipinos to fill all the bomb craters, and smooth the runway surface in order to handle supply planes and fighter planes that moved in and out. With air superiority over the Japanese, the ability to supply troops in the battlefield by air was a distinct advantage in keeping the pressure on a retreating enemy. Lang rounded up the tools and hired locals and their carabao and carts to accomplish the task. Without heavy equipment, the work was completed one shovel at a time. The Filipinos entered into the physical labor with an enthusiasm that made Lang marvel. The advice "to make friends with the natives" proved to pay dividends once more.

PT boats, the seventy-foot long plywood speedboats used to ferry General MacArthur, his family, and his crew from Corregidor to Mindanao, were once again active in the Bahol and Visayan Seas. When first furnished to the Navy the concept was not well received by career navy men, who wanted big, steel battleships. General MacArthur saw their value in the Philippine waters after his famous journey and more boats were added to the inventory of Navy craft. They were particularly successful as couriers, scouts, and torpedo boats in and about the numerous islands in the Philippines where they could be easily concealed and serviced.

In January 1945, Lang completed his work at the airfield and reported to Lieutenant Colonel Childress, his division commander, for his next assignment. Colonel Childress, in a serious tone, said, "Dick, I have received permission from SOUWESPAC to leave the island and return to the United States. In addition, nine other Americans were given permission to return to the United States. Dick, you have a choice. You have permission to return with us or you can stay on here in the islands to continue your splendid work.

Do you want to give it some thought?"

Dick was very fond of Colonel Childress and his directness. After a very, very brief hesitation said, "Sir, I have eaten enough grasshoppers! I would like to join you and leave the island."

Lang dispatched a trusted guerrilla officer to return to headquarters and convey to Waldo Neveling that he would be leaving. Dick and Waldo had accomplished a good deal in their brief association, and each brought special skills to their assignments. Their paths might never cross again, but for a time they were a good team. Lang trusted the German without reservation. He wanted Waldo to know that.

The next morning the eleven men and Ernie started for the north coast, to Cagayan, where there were several PT boats anchored. When they arrived at the port, they made all the arrangements for departure and set their schedule.

Dick and Ernie sat under palm trees on the beach near the docks. They had been together almost two and a half years and faced many hardships, as well as experienced good times. Ernie worked well alongside Lang and was a dedicated soldier as well as personal assistant. Dick truly appreciated Ernie and recognized how valuable he was in working with the natives and the guerrillas. Dick enjoyed Ernie's persistently good humor, took delight in observing Ernie's many love affairs, and appreciated his ability to find food and prepare it. The diminutive mestizo was a close and trusted friend.

Dick proceeded to give Ernie all of his possessions, except for his personal items. He gave him the four or five pistols and revolvers Lang had accumulated during his travels. He handed Ernie his bolo knife, carried on his belt since leaving Clark Field. He gave him his carbine, compass, and clothing he would no longer need. Then Lang stood up and gave Ernie a long hug. With tears in his eyes, he walked to the dock, picked up his near empty duffel bag, and climbed aboard a PT boat.

The eleven men looked back at the island where they had spent over two and a half years of their young lives. The guerrillas split up with five on one boat and six on the other for their trip to Leyte.

They each had experiences difficult to describe and even more perplexing, wondered why fate selected them to experience them. To a man, they were ecstatic to leave the island. To a man, they were too emotional to speak.

The baby-faced PT skipper strolled down the dock, saluted his teenage crew, and jumped aboard his plywood wonder. A sailor responded to the skippers command, and the triple Chrysler marine engines rumbled to life, it's tie lines were coiled and stored on the deck as the boat inched away from the dock into the harbor. As the color of water changed from pale green to dark blue, the skipper pushed the throttles full forward, and the PT boat literally jumped on plane. They suddenly were flying along at fifty miles per hour, bouncing across the open water. The fresh air hit the six soldiers seated on the deck and they gasped for breath as they were caught in the moving air.

The men suddenly realized they were free of the mantle of daily pressures living on a faraway island in a frightening jungle with the constant fear of the next day's perils. The men laughed, then shouted.

They were on their way home.

Chapter Fifteen

THE LONG TRIP HOME

The PT boat's spray swirled around as the two boats skimmed the water at top speed. Traveling north along the Surigao coast, through Surigao Strait and into Leyte Gulf, they occasionally spotted U.S. warships protecting cargo ships. They entered San Pedro Bay and pulled into the docks at Tacloban City on the east shore of Leyte. It was the main support port for the troops fighting in the hills. After the two hundred sixty mile trip bouncing about for six hours, the PT boats pulled alongside makeshift docks well away from the main port area, where there was a beehive of activity. As the guerrillas left the plywood boats they thanked the crews for delivering them from Mindanao safely to Leyte, and crawled aboard a truck headed inland to a tent city.

Their first activity was to check into the personnel tent and then find a mess tent for a warm meal. Assigned a sleeping tent, the officers found the tent and a cot, and proceeded to catch up on their lost sleep. It took awhile to recover from their jarring boat ride. For the first time in years, the men would have three square meals a day, warm showers, sinks and the semblance of toilet paper.

Until a ship returning to the U.S. was available, Lang was assigned the job to censor soldier's letters home. For one long month, Lang rested, censored letters, and readjusted to military life as an officer. Tacloban was the main access for forwarding supplies and ammunition to the troops. The area was in constant motion with ships unloading their cargo and trucks traversing makeshift roads carrying supplies to the interior. It was hot, dusty, and constant, twenty-four hours a day. It was not the only evidence that war was in progress.

The Battle of Surigao Strait was fought on October 15th, when the American navy surprised a Japanese naval task force passing through the straights. As the Japanese vessels passed through the narrow eleven mile opening between the islands, the heavy U.S. war ships proceeded to sink the approaching ships one at a time. Fifty PT boats were lined up on both sides of the exit and did their damage. The U.S. battleships could shoot accurately from twenty miles away, about four miles farther than the Japanese battleships.

Admiral Halsey dispersed his task force to protect Leyte Gulf during the invasion of Leyte. However, the Japanese concocted a plan to lure the task force north. Sending a group of old escort carriers north of Luzon as a decoy, they intended to use a pincher movement with battleships and cruisers passing through San Bernadino Strait and Suriago Strait to trap the landing forces on Leyte while Admiral Halsey's task force was chasing a decoy of six obsolete escort carriers.

When Admiral Halsey took the bait to pursue the Japanese task force three hundred miles further north, the Japanese began to execute their "pincher" movement trapping the U.S. forces. Fortunately, the heroic efforts of two U.S. destroyers who attacked an overwhelming and superior Japanese naval force in Suriago Strait, caused the southern Japanese task force to retreat to the Mindanao Sea. A fierce defense at San Bernadino Strait, by American naval aircraft from several aircraft carriers in the area, sank two Japanese aircraft carriers and several cruisers, and forced the Japanese to withdraw. The separate but connected battles and subsequent losses of naval craft made the Japanese realize they were now losing the naval war, as well as islands, one by one.

The Japanese, however, did manage to substantially damage the U.S. navy. From December 13, 1944 to January 13, 1945, the U.S. navy was attacked by Japanese kamikaze planes sinking twenty-four ships and severely damaged thirty more. After a young

Japanese pilot successfully crashed his damaged airplane into an aircraft carrier in the battle of the Coral Sea, the Japanese leadership decided, in true bushido tradition, that since everyone ultimately dies, it would be "honorable to die for the Emperor." They proceeded to draft and convince a group of young men to sacrifice their lives, teaching them to take off and fly, but not to land, which certainly shortened time spent in their schooling. The kamikazes achieved a good deal of success in the Battle of Leyte Gulf on January 5, 1945, inflicting the greatest losses to the U.S. Navy ever recorded in a single day.

During this period, there was a good deal of activity in the Philippine Islands. On February 8, 1945, General MacArthur's soldiers returned to Manila. The city that was declared an "open city" by the Americans as they retreated in 1942 was totally destroyed by the Japanese as they retreated. Over one hundred thousand Filipino citizens were killed during the Japanese withdrawal. On February 17, American forces recaptured Bataan peninsula. On February 18, American forces invaded Corregidor, where reconnaissance reported there were only six to seven hundred Japanese defenders remaining. The Americans decided to attack by dropping one thousand paratroopers from the 503rd Parachute Infantry Regiment on a very small golf course on top of the mountain, landing one thousand troops on the beach and reinforced them later with an additional one thousand troops. In reality there were seven thousand Japanese troops hidden in the tunnels on the island. Of the one thousand paratroopers who dropped on the island, two hundred ninety-five received broken bones and injuries from landing on the rock surface and bombed out buildings. Vicious fighting continued for two weeks, as the Japanese would sneak out of the tunnels at night to fight the tired out numbered troopers at short range. During the battle, two hundred twenty three troopers were killed, and one thousand one hundred seven troopers were wounded, which was over one-third of the American force. Over seven thousand Japanese died in the battle. Two weeks after fighting ceased, twenty starving and emaciated Japanese soldiers who had survived deep in the tunnel system broke with bushido tradition and surrendered to one American soldier doing cleanup work for grave registration.

On March 2, 1945, General Douglas MacArthur "led an entourage of high brass onto four PT boats for a triumphant return to Corregidor" in a staged landing, accompanied by a score of camera men. Although the return was emotional, the General managed to conceal his feelings as he toured the island, whose topography was irrevocably altered by the bombing and battles. General MacArthur viewed the landscape from his jeep caravan and announced, "Gentlemen, Corregidor is living proof that the day of the fixed fortress is over."

Lang continued to censor soldier's letters at headquarters in Tacloban. However, he received his first wounds in the process. While riding on the back of a truck driving through a makeshift road in the jungle, a large tree branch bounced off the front cab striking Lang on the side of the face, knocking him off the truck. He suffered broken nose and a good deal of dental damage in the form of a broken jaw bone and loosened teeth. He was immediately transported to the infirmary where they tended to his loose teeth and nose. He remained in bed several days with a severe headache.

Finally, in late February he received orders to return to the United States. Once again Lang packed his gear, caught a ride to the docks, and boarded the SS *Monterey*, bound for Finchhaven, New Guinea. Traveling in convoy to New Guinea, the ship docked just long enough to take on additional soldiers. Then, traveling alone, the *Monterey* departed at full speed toward San Francisco.

The *Monterey* was an elegant luxury liner, and the soldiers received treatment they never knew existed. They could eat any hour of the day, anything they wanted, and as much as they wanted. The food was prepared with great flourish, and the soldiers enjoyed being fussed over by the ship's staff. One of the waiters, Greek in origin, served Lang's table, and they became comrades. When the ship arrived in San Francisco the waiter took the entire table to a famous San Francisco restaurant for an evening of drinking and dining, and picked up the tab for everything. He knew what the men had been through and insisted upon showing his appreciation in the grandest manner possible.

Arriving in San Francisco ten days after leaving New Guinea, the men went through processing and a thorough physical. Lang called Margaret to inform her he was on U.S. soil and would be home soon. Receiving travel orders, Lang boarded a Central Pacific train for Ames, Iowa. Arriving in Ames, he walked across Clark Avenue to the Greyhound bus station, and caught the next bus for Des Moines.

As he stepped off the bus, Margaret was waiting, and they hugged for a full five minutes, too joyous to find words. Three years and seven months after their brief honeymoon, they were together again.

The following weeks were a whirlwind of family gatherings, church suppers, and community warmth. Everyone wanted to see the young soldier in person, and to hear of his experiences. The "Marshalltown Times Republican" and the "Des Moines Register and Tribune" both interviewed him and made Lang front-page news. The war was nearing an end, and his story would be the first of many articles about returning service men and women.

After two weeks of local activities, Lang entered Schick Military Hospital in Clinton, Iowa, for a two month visit. After a thorough physical examination, be began treatment for a serious infestation of "hookworm" that he had been entertaining for probably over a year. The treatment was long and the medicine "tasted awful." Since the head of the worms would attach to intestine walls and regenerate, the treatment amounted to getting the worm in a relaxed state through inebriation, so it was too relaxed to reattach. At least that is how the story goes.

Lang also was able to get some dental reconstruction from the tree limb damage while at Schick Hospital. Two years without brushing and an inconsistent diet also had taken their toll. Lang felt the dentist's drill often, and deep.

After their two-months of treatment in Clinton, Iowa, Dick and Margaret enjoyed six months of accumulated leave. It was their opportunity to get to know each other, become reacquainted with their families, and start a family of their own.

Lang returned to Santa Ana, California for reassignment. While in the Schick Hospital he met and became friends with a soldier named Bridges who lived on a ranch in California. It turned out that Bridges also owned a house on the beach at Coronado Del Mar, and offered to let the Lang's use it while they were in California awaiting reassignment. For two months, November and December 1946, Margaret and Dick enjoyed watching the sun go down over the Pacific Ocean.

Lang received orders to report to Wright Field in Dayton, Ohio. The family piled into their new 1947 Buick Special and drove to Dayton. Initially the Army intended to send him to Engineering Officers School. His orders changed, however, and he attended Finance Officers School in Indianapolis, Indiana for six months. Lang then returned to Wright Field, for reassignment. He was faced with a decision to remain in service or be discharged. Promoted to Captain, Lang was given an opportunity to become finance officer at an airbase in Tokyo, Japan, for a two-year tour of duty.

Dick approached Margaret with the option to become a military wife, enjoy world travel, and an opportunity to live in Japan. Margaret did not hesitate for a second. "You mean you just spent three and a half years in the jungle being shot at by the Japanese, and now you want to go over and spend two more years living with them? Not only am I not going, but you are not going either. Three and a half years away is enough!" It was not quite the response Dick had expected.

While overseas, Dick had accumulated a nest egg of four or five thousand dollars in accumulated pay. Perhaps Margaret was not cut out for military life. He had been a soldier for almost ten years, including his National Guard days. Perhaps it was time to return to Iowa far a more stable future. Dick decided to leave the service.

In July 1947, Capt. Dick Lang formally separated from the U.S. Army Air Corps.

Chapter Sixteen

LIFE AFTER SERVICE

Returning to Iowa, Margaret and Dick Lang now traveled with two young children. This would certainly help dictate where and how they would place their roots. Margaret's parents operated a farmstead near Zearing IA, and were considering retirement. Dick and Margaret recognized the opportunity and decided to become tenant farmers. They rented the one hundred sixty acre homestead, and contracted to farm an additional one hundred twenty acres. Dick's military pay nest egg was used to acquire new field equipment and a new International Harvester Tractor.

Dick Lang aboard his first tractor, an International Harvester Farmall M. 1948.

A family was started while Dick was stationed in Dayton, Ohio. Judy Marie was born on March 11, 1946. The Langs proceeded to expand their family:

Marcia Rose was born July 10, 1947

Michael Anthony was born July 2, 1949

Patrick Alan was born September 7, 1950

Louis Ambrose was born April 2, 1953

And John Richard joined the family on February 9, 1956.

Another child, Mary Katherine, died three days after her birth.

The Lang Family celebrating Margaret and Dick's twenty-fifth wedding anniversary, September 1966. Left to right: Marcia, Judy, Patrick, Dick, John, Margaret, Louis and Michael.

A house full of children kept Margaret and Dick on the run. They still managed to keep active in church and school activities. All the children attended the school system in Zearing, Iowa. The family ultimately included eighteen grandchildren and seven great grandchildren

Dick and Margaret continued to farm until 1978, when they decided to retire. In 1973 Margaret received a recognition from Robert Lounsberry, of the Iowa Department of Agriculture, saluting

Margaret Carmody Lang for working a family farm for over fifty years. Consistent with common practice in Iowa, the Langs had a farm sale, selling their farming equipment at auction. Several hundred neighbors attended, some interested in acquiring farm equipment, and others interested in the free coffee and sandwiches. Leaving the farm is always bitter sweet, but moving to a new home at 1510 Curtis Avenue in Ames, Iowa was a new beginning for the farm couple.

Dick became quite active in both the American Guerrillas of Mindanao (AGOM) veterans group and the National Organization of Battlefield Commissions, known as the "Mustangs." Dick and Margaret attended a number of reunions, where casual acquaintances in the middle of the jungle became close friends once stateside. Dick served as president of AGOM for two years, and arranged for Des Moines to host the national convention in 1987. The reunion was attended by fifty veterans and their wives who re-lived shared experiences of thirty years ago. Dick's daughter Marcia edited the AGOM newsletter for two years.

At the reunion of AGOM in San Diego in the early 1990's, Lang saw an attractive woman sitting at the far end of the banquet room. Dick approached her and asked, "Are you a lady I met on Mindanao?" The woman replied, "My name is Glenda Kreitzer. Are you the gentleman who arranged for me to leave the island by submarine?" The two spent several hours reflecting on their experiences in the Philippine Islands. Glenda's husband, taken prisoner

Attendees at the reunion of the American Guerrillas of Mindanao in Park CA, June 1984.

in Davao and forced to run the dock system there, survived the war, and the family was reunited in 1946.

Dick heard several times about the travels of Waldo Neveling from a variety of sources, but was never in direct contact with him. They had worked very closely for over two years and shared a number of life threatening experiences. Waldo became a very close friend

Colonel Eubanks and Dick Lang attending a reunion of the American Guerrillas of Mindanao, November 1982.

of Lieutenant Bob Spielman from Texas, and visited him frequently. Spielman married an American/Filipino mestizo who had lost two brothers while fighting with the guerrillas. After the war was over Waldo went to Central America to consult with gold mining companies about water control in mines. He later went to Spain and traveled Eastern Europe. Because of his service in the Philippine Islands he exercised his opportunity to become an American citizen. Waldo's major failing was his constant smoking, which seemed to bother his friends a good deal. It proved to be his demise. He died from emphysema while living in Texas and is buried there.

Dick never had any additional contact with "Filipino adjutant" Earnesto "Ernie" Lancen. Ernie's sister married an American soldier and came to the United States. The cultural change proved to be too great, and she returned to her home in the Philippine Islands. With Ernie's success with the dalagas in every small town, one would presume that he lived as a contented satiated soldier, or was shot by a jealous husband.

Dick continues to remark on the unique characteristics of the Filipino people who meant so much to him during his service experience. General Douglas MacArthur commented specifically about the character of the Filipinos. The General appreciated "(1) their enduring fortitude and courage and patriotic self-abnegation; (2) Their love of life—treating the world as a playground; and (3) Their hospitality-cordially, but generosity sometime carried too far." These are qualities Dick Lang found in abundance, and still appreciates to this day.

For his service experience Dick Lang received a number of accolades and medals. He received two Bronze Stars, the Philippine Government Award of Military Merit, The National Defense Medal and the Asiatic-Pacific Theater Ribbon.

At a ceremony at the Ames Legion Hall on March 22, 2003, Dick Lang received a medal commemorating the National Order of Battlefield Commissions, No. 550 R. B. Lang (Mustangs) World War II.

The medal is a fitting tribute for a small town Iowa boy who met the challenge of surviving in a difficult environment in a distant land, under unusual circumstances.

Richard B. Lang rolled up his sleeves and met those challenges with distinction.

Dick Lang (with wife, Margaret) receiving a medal commemorating the National Order of Battlefield Commissions, No. 550 R. B. Lang (Mustangs) World War II.

Sylvester and Anna Lang and Margaret and Dick inspect a scrapbook kept by Margaret while Dick was in the Philippines.

Dick and Margaret taken when Dick first returned from overseas. 1945.

**HEADQUARTERS
EIGHTH UNITED STATES
ARMY**

Citation

The Commanding General, Eighth Army, in Section III, General Orders No. 84, 24 July 1945, cites and awards a Bronze Star Medal to:

First Lieutenant RICHARD B. LANG, Infantry, United States Forces in the Philippines. For meritorious achievement in connection with military operations against the enemy on Mindanao, Philippine Islands, from 1 May 1944 to 1 January 1945. Lieutenant Lang displayed outstanding initiative and ingenuity in establsihing repair facilities for the motor launches of the Tenth Military District. He skillfully rebuilt a machine shop and fitted it with necessary tools for servicing marine craft. The launches were used to carry food and ammunition to guerrilla troops and were of vital importance in sustaining opposition against the Japanese. The contribution which Lieutenant Lang made in aiding guerrilla resistance reflects great credit on himself and on the military service. Home address: Mrs. Richard B. Lang (Wife), Route #2, Marshalltown, Iowa.

The citation for Dick Lang's first Bronze Star Medal.

Memorial Day Service circa 1960. Tom Davis, Harlow McBride, Dick Lang, Lee Meredith

GLOSSARY OF FILIPINO TERMS

abaca – a hemp plant grown for fibers for making rope.

banca – a boat or launch with a motor and a sail.

barrios – a small village, or makeshift housing.

baroto – a small boat or canoe, usually with an outrigger for stability.

bolo – an eighteen inch or longer machete.

caba caba – a very small canoe or banca.

camote – a sweet potato.

camote in kahoy – a tree root, made edible by cooking.

carabao – a variety of the water buffalo.

chibasco – a wall of rain with very high winds.

copra – dried meat from a coconut, processed for oil, soap, perfume, and other products.

coogan – a coarse grass growing three feet to eight foot high. (also called cogon)

cotare – a cocktail or drink.

dalagas – a beautiful, single, young girl.

kalibo – a large variety of the banana family, about eighteen inches long and flat.

kalamasi – a fruit similar to a mango.

lechon – roasted suckling pig, served at most gatherings.

mestizo – literally a "half breed." Half Filipino and half other; originally Spanish, but now including American, Chinese, Indian, Japanese, Portuguese, etc.

obud – the edible top growth of a palm tree.

Salamat po – thank you.

swalley – woven bamboo panels, used for separation walls.

Taglog – a major dialect of the Philippine language.

tuba – fermented sap from a palm tree.

Visian – a dialect of the Philippine language.

SOME IMPORTANT DATES:
1941

Dec 8, 1941   Japanese bomb Philippines and Pearl Harbor (Dec. 7th Same date).

Dec 10, 1941 Japanese invade Philippines on Luzon, Leyte and Mindoro.

1942

Jan 2, 1942   Japanese occupy Manila

Feb 15, 1942 Singapore falls

Mar 9, 1942   Japanese overrun Java and Burma's capitol, Rangoon, falls.

Mar 16, 1942 War Department announces "considerable numbers"of US troops have arrived in Australia. (actually, a piddly amount).

Mar 17 1942   Gen. Douglas MacArthur reaches Australia from the Philippines.

Mar 31, 1942 Japanese begin heavy attacks on Bataan.

Apr 9, 1942   Fighting ends on Bataan.

May 6, 1942   Corregidor surrenders.
All troops in the Philippines to surrender.

Jun 12, 1942 Japanese land on Aleutian Islands USA (Attu and Kiska).

Jun 22, 1942 Japanese submarine shells Oregon coast.

Aug 8, 1942   Americans land on Guadalcanal.

1943

May 30, 1943 Japanese garrison on Attu wiped out.

Aug 15, 1943 US forces occupy Kiska (Aleutians).

Nov 21, 1943 US forces land on Makin and Tarawa Islands.

Dec 16, 1943 US forces make surprise landing on New Britain.

1944

Jan 31, 1944	US amphibious forces invade Marshall Islands at Kwajalein.
June 14, 1944	American troops land on Saipan Island in the Marianas, 1,496 miles from Tokyo.
July 20, 1944	US assault troops land on Guam, south of Saipan, 1,596 miles from Tokyo.
Oct 15, 1944	Naval battle of Leyte Gulf
Nov 5, 1944	MacArthur announces that six Japanese divisions were crushed in the Luzon Invasion. Only mopping up operations left (Still battling 27,000 Japanese dug in the mountains.)

1945

Jan 5, 1945	Japanese kamikaze planes inflict severe damage on US Navy ships.
Feb 8, 1945	MacArthur returns to Manila; Japanese set fire to the city.
Feb 17, 1945	Recapture of historic Bataan in the Philippines: Corregidor invaded the next day.
Feb 21, 1945	Opposition ends on Corregidor
Mar 2, 1945	General MacArthur returns to tour Corregidor.
Mar 11, 1945	Yanks invade Mindanao, second major island of the Philippines.
Mar 17, 1945	Iwo Jima falls to Americans.
Mar 17, 1945	American naval planes hit Japanese fleet in Inland Sea.
Aug 6, 1945	Atomic bomb dropped on Hiroshima
Aug 9, 1945	Atomic bomb dropped on Nagasaki
Aug 14, 1945	V-J Day as Japan surrenders
Sept 2, 1945	Formal surrender signed aboard the USS Missouri in Tokyo Harbor.

ACKNOWLEDGEMENTS

John Klienschmidt first called attention to the unique story of Dick Lang. John, a World War II veteran, has encouraged many veterans to share their experiences with young people in school environments. John is an accomplished writer himself.

Don Mangels, (Colonel-USAF-Retired) read a rough manuscript and made several suggestions to aid in relating Dick Lang's story. His Masters Degree in History from the University of Oklahoma is still in fine form.

Ann Andrews Rudi's quiet encouragement and critical eye helped to define another writing effort. Her patience, understanding, and support are truly appreciated. And, after three writing efforts, she is still my lovely wife.

The editorial staff at McMillen Publishing, Inc. is always a pleasure to work with. We'll try to keep doing this until we get it right!

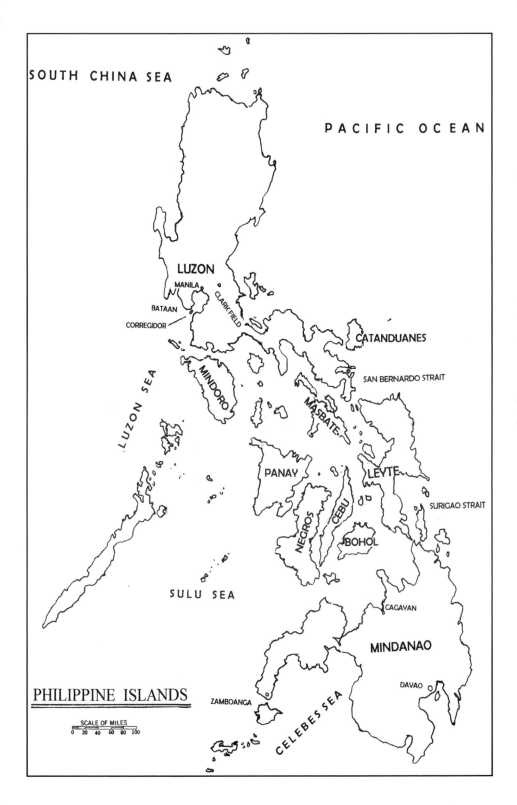

SOUTH CHINA SEA

PACIFIC OCEAN

LUZON

MANILA

BATAAN

CORREGIDOR

CLARK FIELD

CATANDUANES

SAN BERNARDO STRAIT

LUZON SEA

MINDORO

MASBATE

PANAY

LEYTE

SURIGAO STRAIT

NEGROS

CEBU

BOHOL

SULU SEA

CAGAYAN

MINDANAO

DAVAO

PHILIPPINE ISLANDS

SCALE OF MILES

0 20 40 60 80 100

ZAMBOANGA

CELEBES SEA

RESOURCES

American Guerrilla in the Philippines
Ira Wolfort
Simon Schuster 1945
Kingsport Press Inc.
(Lang is mentioned on page 147)

Guerrilla Padre on Mindanao
Edward Haggerty
Longmans Green & Co.
New York-Toronto 1946

The War in the Pacific
Harry A. Gailey
Presidio Press 1995

Retaking the Philippines
William Breuer
St Martins Press 1986

Corregidor
Lt. General E.M. Flanagan
Presidio Press 1988
31 Pamaron Way
Novato CA 94949

Japan's War-the Great Pacific Conflict
William P. Hoyt
McGraw Hill 1986
(An excellent book from a historical standpoint)

Readers Digest – World War II
Readers Digest Association Inc.
Pleasantville NY 1969

Too Young To Die
Carlyle G. Townswick
Privately Published 1979

The Philippines in Pictures
Oak Tree Press 1966
London

Life Nature Library – The Forests
Life Time Inc 1961-1963

I Survived the Shiniyo Maru Sinking Sept.7, 1944
Lyle G. Knudson
Privately Published 03-15-96

Interviews with Moriel Salvadore Aquino Moothart
Born on Catanduanes Island, Philippine Islands
Maternal Grandfather Francisco Salvadore died on the
    Bataan Death March

ABOUT THE AUTHOR

Norman Rudi has long been interested in World War II experiences, since he had three brothers who each served five years exposed to the worst conditions of the conflagration.

Rudi is a WW II veteran who served twenty months as a paratrooper in the 11th Airborne Division in the Army of Occupation in Japan, after hostilities ceased and before the Korean War started.

Rudi was born and raised in Glidden, Iowa. He graduated from the University of Oklahoma where he received a Bachelor of Architecture degree. He worked for two architectural firms in Cedar Rapids, Iowa, before moving to Ames, Iowa, where he was an Associate Professor of Architecture at Iowa State University. He taught full time for six years and part time for seven years. Rudi opened an architectural practice in Ames, Iowa, in 1966 and retired from active practice in 1996.

Active in community organizations, he has served as president of the Ames Society for the Arts, The Ames Chamber of Commerce, The Ames/Story County Cyclone Club, Ames Rotary Club, Ames Golf and Country Club, the Iowa Architectural Examination Board, and served on the Board of Directors of the National Association of Architectural Registration Boards for three years.

Norman is married to the former Ann Andrews of Iowa City, IA. They have two children: Daughter Ann Michelle and her husband Brian Rupiper and children Lauren and Nathan live in Memphis, Tennessee. Son Chris and his wife Paula live in Draper, Utah, where Chris is a PGA Professional.

Norman Rudi's first writing effort, An Iowa Pilot Named Hap, was the biography of Hartley "Hap" Westbrook, a decorated WWII pilot, prisoner of war, airport operator for over fifty years, member of the Iowa Aviation Hall of Fame, and recognized with a National Aeronautics Association Elder Statesman of Aviation Award. Rudi's second book, A Neighborhood of Eagles, relates the WWII military experiences of nine pilots, bombardiers and navigators, who are his neighbors in Ames, Iowa.

Since retirement in 1996, Rudi spends time reading and writing, golfing with friends, cheering at Big XII sporting events, and watching his grandchildren grow up.